Y0-EKS-733

Praise for SEE YOU IN THE SKY

When I started reading *See You in the Sky*, I didn't want to put it down. I even found myself reading slower than my normal pace, so it would last longer. Stories like Jeri's are such precious jewels for all of us because they remind us to look back at how our choices influenced our lives. *See You in the Sky* shows us how to apply that knowledge to grow in wisdom. There are so many fantastic life experiences in this story. I hope you can recognize them all and they help you in your life, but if you only take one thing away from reading this memoir, your life will be better for it.

—*Harvey RV Powers, currently incarcerated, created and teaches the following courses: Quantum Physics: The Science of Success; Positive Attitude Development: True Colors*

This book sheds light on the tragic consequences of mass incarceration in the United States for families and children. —*Lonnie King III*

Millions of children in this country have a parent in prison. While each child's situation is unique, this tender, easy-to-read memoir captures the common threads of fierce love, loyalty, and longing. I wish *See You in the Sky* had been available when I began my work with children and families of the incarcerated thirty years ago. This healing resource shares a much-needed message about love beyond bars.

—*Sandra Kay Barnhill, JD, Founder and CEO of Foreverfamily*

I raised my own two children from prison. As a recently released Obama clemency recipient who was incarcerated for twenty-three years, I needed Jeri's book. It inspired me to want to know more about how my incarceration impacted my children. Her story helped me to put myself in my children's shoes, to see things from their point of view for the first time.

See You in the Sky confirms for me what I long suspected: I am responsible for my own happiness and sorrow. I create my own peace within.

—*Glenn L. Williams, Educator, Screenwriter, Independent Producer, Workforce Development Director*

See You in the Sky is a daughter's journey from a childhood of chaos, trauma, and shame to an adulthood of healing and peace.

Jeri Ross shares the raw truth of her life as the child of an incarcerated father. Hers is a story shared by millions of children. Jeri's search for spiritually healthy responses to life's greatest challenges becomes a guide, not just for the children of the incarcerated, but for all of us as we reconcile our relationships with our parents.

—Susan Latina, Program Coordinator, Get on the Bus/Uniting Children with their Incarcerated Parents, Center for Restorative Justice Works

As the mother of an incarcerated daughter, and a grandmother raising her grandchildren, I am inspired by *See You in the Sky*.

Jeri's book shows the other side of incarceration: the human stories from families who get pulled into tragic situations. Her story shows how we cope, survive, heal, forgive, love and refuse to give up on our loved ones. Jeri offers all of us a gift of hope.

—Christina Garrett, Caregiver Advocacy Project

See You in the Sky is a gripping account of one woman's journey to heal from the confusion, shame and loss of having her father in prison for most of her life.

Her memoir underscores the value of mentorship for youth that have experienced family trauma, and the importance of providing them with the guidance they need to prevent incarceration, drug addiction and poverty. Jeri practices what she preaches: When I was eighteen, she reached out and helped me to attend college and land my first career job in health education. She saw potential in me to become the community leader I am today.

—Gina Castaneda, Santa Cruz County Juvenile Probation Officer; Founder and Head Coach, Aztecas Youth Soccer Academy; American Red Cross Lifetime Achievement Hero

See You in the Sky

A Memoir of Prison,
Possibility and Peace

JERI ROSS

Copyright © 2019 Jeri Ross

All rights reserved. This book or any portion thereof may not be reproduced or used in any manner whatsoever without the express written permission of the publisher except for the use of brief quotations in a book review.

Library of Congress Control Number: 2019914222

ISBN 978-7332953-0-7 (softcover)
ISBN 978-7332953-1-4 (ebook)

Edited by Maggie de Vries
Design by Teresa Bubela
Cover photos by evakad17/Shutterstock.com
Author photo by Devi Pride Photography

Panther Press cares for the environment and has chosen to print this book on paper that is 100% post-consumer recycled.

PANTHER PRESS
Jeri Ross
PO Box 3419
Santa Cruz, CA 95062

seeyouintheskythebook.com

Printed and bound in Canada

10 9 8 7 6 5 4 3 2 1

For my mother, my father
and families of the incarcerated

Contents

PART III

2000–2018

So moments pass as though
they wished to stay.
We have not long to love.
A night. A day …

— Tennessee Williams

Foreword

In the eleven years I've been training life coaches, I've worked with hundreds of students. A few have made powerful impressions and left clear memories. Jeri Ross is one of those.

When she appeared in one of my classes five years ago, I could see that she was in pain. Her aging, beloved father was serving a life sentence without possibility of parole for drug trafficking. She longed for his release. Her admitting her feelings to a group of people she barely knew impressed me right at the start.

In one memorable class, Jeri volunteered to work with me so I could demonstrate how to coach using The Work of Byron Katie, a powerful method that helps relieve stress and anxiety caused by painful thoughts that may not be true.

As we began to work together, her honesty and vulnerability were immediately apparent. And over the next thirty minutes or so, her extraordinary courage surfaced. The class and I watched her let go of the illusion that she needed her father to be released from prison so that she could live happily and be free of suffering. It was a stunning exchange and I never forgot it.

See You in the Sky tells the story of Jeri's relationship with her father, but it's about so much more than that. Yes, it's the story of a young girl, then woman, with a special and loving relationship with a man who didn't always behave well. But beyond that, it's the story of how she healed her relationship with her father through her candor and authenticity. It's the story of how she found forgiveness. And it's the story of how we human beings can rise, we can awaken, and we can face great challenges with dignity and resilience.

This book will be an invaluable guide and inspiration for families of the incarcerated. It can also help any of us who have been raised by dysfunctional parents. Jeri tells a powerful story of love and loss and forgiveness and how she came to heal by facing the truth and having courageous, authentic conversations. It's much easier to talk about such authenticity than it is to live it. Jeri's story provides a clear map of healing—something that can benefit most all of us.

Terry DeMeo, JD
Master Certified Coach
Personal and Professional Development
October, 2019

Prologue

Can that woman in the mirror be me? That woman artfully applying red lipstick in the washroom at Le Méridien Etoile, mere blocks from the Champs-Élysées? Can she be me, French chic in a white linen pencil skirt, black sleeveless ribbed top and knee-high suede boots?

"Voila!" I say, and the woman in the armoire mirror twirls right along with me, ready at last for one of the biggest days of my life. I slip my arms into my sleek black trench coat, belt it at the waist and leave the hotel.

My taxi drops me at Colette, a high fashion boutique on the Rue Saint-Honoré in the 1st arrondissement. I take a deep breath, walk up to the front door and pull. It's locked. My shoulders tense. Can I somehow have gotten the date wrong? Then, to my relief, the door cracks open. I step back. A thin, unsmiling woman peers out and says something to me in French. The only thing I know to do is reply in English.

"I'm here from America for the press event to launch my line of women's body care products."

"*Oui, oui, oui,*" she says, ushering me in and down a flight of stairs to a small, colorful café. My shoulders relax when I see Delphine, my international marketing agent, whom I first met in New York City, talking to an attractive woman a few yards away.

"Jeri!" she calls out as they walk toward me. We give one another the customary European greeting, a small kiss on each cheek.

"I want to introduce you to Natalie," Delphine says. "She's put so much work into the new packaging designs."

Natalie and I perform the kiss, kiss ritual. "Jeri, I am so thrilled to finally meet you. It has been my honor to work with your brand," she says in English, her accent thick.

I blink several times, trying to comprehend how I got here. In awe I reach out and touch her hand. "Natalie, I could not have done this without you and Delphine. Now my success is your success."

The morning unfolds. I am interviewed by leading magazine beauty editors and photographed next to the store's displays of my products. By late afternoon my feet ache, so I walk over to sit on a tufted gray leather couch against the far wall. As I relax, my mind fills with an image of my father.

"Dad!" I say to him inside my head. "Can you believe our products are in Paris? You would be so amazed by all of this!"

Natalie comes over and sits next to me. She looks me straight in the eye. "Jeri," she says, "I wish to know the story about how you developed your products. Not the technical part, but the story."

My face flushes. I haven't prepared myself for this question. I have secrets. I can't possibly tell her everything. I certainly can't let her know that much of the product formulation was conceived in the visiting room of a maximum-security federal prison.

1

From the Beginning

The way I see it, the story that led to the press appearance in Paris began many years earlier. Decades earlier, in fact, when I was six and my sister, Lyn, was seven.

We lived on Alverado Way in Decatur, Georgia. My best memories from that time are of how much Lyn and I loved playing with our daddy. We would lie on Daddy's bed with our shaking legs sticking straight up in the air, trying to balance pillows on our feet. We were getting ready for the bomber plane to drop its bombs, with Daddy's fingers poised to tickle our ribs with direct hits. Our job was to hold him off with our legs.

"Here come the bombs!" Daddy warned us, leaning his heavy body into the pillows.

We squealed with delight, pushing as hard as we could to keep him far enough away that his fingers couldn't reach us. But it never worked.

"Rat-a-tat! Rat-a-tat-tat!" he shouted, poking our sides until we were weak from laughing.

When our tired legs dropped to the bed and the pillows fell off, I would scream, "Do it again, Daddy! Play bomber again!" And he would, over and over, until Mommy called out that it was time to get ready for bed.

MY SISTER AND I SHARED a bedroom in a small brick house that my parents bought for $14,000 in 1957 when I was four. Our two single beds were supposed to be bunk beds, but they were pushed against the walls on each side of the room. There was just enough space for us to maneuver between them when it was time to go to sleep. It also meant that when we climbed up on the dresser and soared off, pretending we could fly like Superman, we would land safely on either bed.

Some nights I would lie in my little bed and wait until I heard my sister's breathing get deeper and deeper. I would sit up, quiet as could be, touch my bare feet to the floor and tiptoe to the door. I could hear the TV and I knew that Daddy would be watching his favorite show, *The Untouchables*, about a detective named Eliot Ness who had shootouts with gangsters.

With both hands, I turned the doorknob ever so carefully and pushed until light cascaded through the opening. Holding my breath, I stepped through and closed the door behind me. Muffled voices from the TV got louder and louder as I walked from the hall into the living room, where I stood holding my satin blanket and rubbing my eyes until my daddy spoke to me.

"Hey, Pumpkin. What are you doing? I thought you were sleeping."

Blinking hard, I peered at him, sitting in his chair across the room. "I can't sleep, Daddy," I said, making my voice as sweet as it could be.

"You can't sleep? Okay, come on over here, Ber."

My family nickname was Jer Ber (pronounced "bear"), but mostly I was just called Ber.

As I approached, he reached for me and pulled me gently onto his lap, where I pressed my face against his warm chest. He would hold me in his arms like that even after my mommy came in and caught me.

"Jeri, what are you doing in here? You're supposed to be sleeping," she'd say, her eyebrows all scrunched together.

"I can't sleep, Mommy," I would whimper.

"She's okay. Let her stay up for a little while," Daddy told her.

Mommy would turn and go back into the kitchen, and I would push closer into the warmth of my daddy's soft body, drifting off, so that all I remembered the next day was waking for a brief moment as he lay me in my bed.

I LOVED WADING IN the muddy creek that ran under an old wooden bridge just down the street. I thrilled at resting in the branches high up in one of the spindly pine trees in our yard, and I was enraptured by the allure of adventure when my sister let me follow her into the thick forest that spread out behind the row of houses along the creek banks. Sometimes

I thought I saw leprechauns hiding underneath the kudzu vines along the shadowy path. At dusk on hot, humid summer evenings I caught fireflies under the mimosa trees and put them in mason jars with lids my mommy had punched holes in with an ice pick.

I was fascinated by the dramatic eruption of summer storms. Bewitched, Lyn and I would lie side by side on our driveway, wearing nothing but T-shirts and underwear, watching bolts of lightning burst across the sky. We would count together, "One, two, three," until a clap of thunder sent us squealing up the driveway and under the carport just ahead of the downpour.

Mom wanted my sister and me to have many diverse experiences. She enrolled us in ballet, ice-skating and library book clubs. She believed in the value and promise of education, instilling in me a passion for lifelong learning.

When I was only five, she talked our next-door neighbor into giving me piano lessons. Two days a week I would take my music book, cross the crabgrass in our front yard and knock on Mrs. Montgomery's door.

"Come in, Jeri," she would say in her deep, gravelly voice. Against the far wall of her living room was her Cable-Nelson piano.

After I got settled and opened my book to the song I was practicing, she rasped, "Let's hear you play 'This Old Man.'"

My chubby, child fingers plucked out the notes, first with one hand, then the other.

"Very good, Jeri. You know what that means."

My legs swung back and forth under the piano bench as she held out a small cardboard box, lifted the lid and let me choose a gold star. I stuck out my tongue, licked the glue on the back of the star and pressed it onto the page of my book. When I didn't feel like practicing, the thought of how Mrs. Montgomery praised me and gave me a gold star roused me to do it anyway.

Not long after I started lessons, my parents bought me my very own piano. We crammed it into the dining room along with our lazy Susan table and console record player. When the repetitive notes from my practicing weren't wafting through the house, Mom would play her favorite records, Ella Fitzgerald, Benny Goodman, Perry Como and Nat King Cole.

Dad always listened to Mario Lanza, an opera singer who kind of resembled Dad, with his thick black wavy hair and fine, handsome features. Mom told me that when she and Dad were dating, they went to see a Mario Lanza movie, and that's how Dad first discovered the famous tenor. When Dad heard him sing "Be My Love," he told my mom that was their song.

One of my favorite songs was "High Hopes," sung by Frank Sinatra. It was about an ant who hoped to move a rubber tree plant. My sister and I would go around the house singing, "*He's got high hopes, he's got high apple pie in the sky hopes … Oops, there goes another rubber tree plant!*" When I was little, Dad was a Permastone salesman, and when he built a Permastone planter box on our living room wall, we filled it with rubber tree plants.

Mom and Dad the day they eloped in 1951.

SHORTLY AFTER MY seventh birthday, Mom told me that Dad had a new job. He was now a bail bondsman.

"What's that?" I asked her.

"Well, when someone does something against the law and they're put in jail, a bondsman helps them get out until they go to court," she said.

"Oh," I said, not understanding but feeling like it didn't really matter.

What did matter was that now Daddy was gone more. When I asked Lyn why, she told me that he was out trying to catch people who got out of jail and ran away.

At my first piano recital, Mom saved a seat for Daddy, but he never showed up.

However, when he had the urge to be with us—his "two-both," as he affectionately referred to Lyn and me—he would appear, with no regard for where we were, to take us out for joyrides in the car or even to nightclubs. Kids weren't allowed in the clubs, but there Lyn and I would be, sitting at the bar drinking Shirley Temples while Dad had important business meetings. He told us that he got us from a pet store and that we were his pets. I guess to him that meant we for sure belonged to him.

Me and my sister, dressed up to go out with our daddy.

One day my second-grade teacher, Miss Campbell, was having us take turns reading out loud in our *See Spot Run* books when I heard a soft knock. I looked up from my desk and saw my dad's face peering through the small square window in the closed classroom door. Miss Campbell's gaze followed the kids' stares to the door. Just then I saw him see me. His eyes widened and he nodded his head.

I sat motionless. By this time, Miss Campbell had walked across the room and was opening the door.

"Can I help you?" she asked, a bewildered tone in her voice.

"Yes, you can," Dad answered with his best beguiling smile. "I'm here to get my daughter Jeri."

Every pair of eyes in the classroom, including Miss Campbell's, turned to me.

"Is this your father?" she asked.

"Yes, ma'am," I whispered. No other father had ever appeared like this, asking to take his child out of school. I was so confused because when I left with my mom to go to the dentist, I had to give the teacher a note from Mom asking permission.

"It's all right for you to go with him, then," Miss Campbell said, turning back to Dad with a troubled look.

When I got out in the hallway and shut the classroom door, Dad took my hand. "Let's go have more fun than being in school!" he said. Lyn stood beside him, already collected from her classroom. And off we went downtown to his bonding company.

My sister and me at our dad's bail bonding company in 1960.

Our father started his bail bonding company across from the Atlanta city jail in 1960. He told my sister and me that even though we were just children, his dream was that his two-both would take over the bonding company someday. He would kneel down, put his arms around our waists and say with a rosy voice, "You girls will have the biggest bonding company in Atlanta and you'll be rich. That's what I want for my girls, only the best."

As I remember it, the bonding company consisted of one massive, dusty room containing nothing but a couple of metal filing cabinets and two scratched-up wooden desks with black dial phones sitting on them. For fun, Dad would tell Lyn and me to stand up against the bare beige wall and pose for mug shots, just like the ones he took of the criminals he bonded out of jail.

"Stand real still," he'd say, holding up a Polaroid camera. The camera clicked and spit out a black-and-white square paper Dad called a snapshot. Lyn and I ran over to watch our faces appear like magic on the shiny paper as he explained, "It's still developing."

One day he took us across the street to the jail.

"Let's go eat," he said. He took my hand and walked Lyn and me right up to a spooky-looking old stone building with bars in the windows. I shuddered when a steel door buzzed, slowly slid open and clanked shut after we passed through. I held my daddy's hand tighter and tighter as he guided us down a musty, dimly lit hallway and stopped to knock on a large gray door.

"Come on, girls. I want you to meet some friends of mine," he said as that door slid open. He led us into a large room with TV screens on the walls and men in blue uniforms sitting behind desks.

One after another, "Harold, how y'all doin'?" the guards said to our daddy, spitting brown tobacco juice out the side of their mouths into dirty coffee cans.

"Good, good," he replied to each of them. "These are my two-both, Lyn and Jeri. We're going to eat lunch with all of you. Right, girls?"

Mute, I stared at the gigantic, burly guards and huddled in closer against my daddy's legs. I was starting to think that I didn't want to grow up and be rich if it meant I had to eat with these scary men in this scary building.

Sometimes Daddy took us to the courthouse. I was just learning to read, and one day I noticed the signs that were posted over the water coolers in the lobby.

"*Colored, White,*" I sounded out. "What does that mean, Daddy?"

His eyes narrowed. "First of all, I want you to know that I don't agree with these signs. It's not right. It means that people with brown, colored skin have their own fountains and white people have theirs." He picked me up by the waist so I could take a drink from the fountain under the *White* sign. That was the first time growing up in the South I learned that black people were treated differently from white people.

The next time was when I was in third grade. Until then there were only white kids at Midway Elementary. I wasn't sure why, but now some black boys and girls were bused in to the school. Just like my dad saying that it wasn't right to have separate drinking fountains, I didn't feel right teasing the new kids. But that didn't stop some of my schoolmates from calling them names like Bosco, a chocolate syrup I poured on my ice cream.

2

Sticker Bushes

Another thing that happened when I was eight years old, I saw Daddy get very mad for the first time.

"God dammit, Joan!" Dad screamed at our mom one night at dinner. He had just arrived home after being out of town, he told us, trying to catch one of those criminals that had run away.

He threw his glass of milk right past my head. The sound of glass shattering filled my ears. My heart hammered inside my chest.

"How many times do I have to tell you that my milk has to be cold?"

No one said a word. Mom, Lyn and I sat there like statues.

Dad got up from the table and stormed into his room.

When I could finally make words come out of my mouth, I said, "Mom, can I be excused? I want to play outside for a while before it gets dark."

Without waiting for a reply, I jumped out of my chair and ran through the kitchen and out the back door into the cool evening air. I ran down the street and hid under the wooden bridge, afraid to go home until I heard my mom calling me.

The next day Dad was in a better mood. He kissed me on the cheek as he went out the door to work and told me that he would be back in a few days with a present for me. My sister and I went to school like always and played outside with our friends.

A week or so later, when Dad was back from working, I was with him in his room, on the bed, coloring in my horse coloring book. He was on the phone. After he hung up, he went over to his closet and pulled on the door handle. It was stuck. He shook it really hard, but it still didn't open. He left and minutes later returned with an ax. I let go of the crayon I was holding and pushed myself back against the wall.

"God dammit!" he shouted. He gripped the ax hard, swung it back and slammed it into the closet door.

Trembling, too frightened to move and barely breathing, I watched him until he dropped the ax, put his arm through the jagged hole he had made, and opened the door.

Over the next several months, Dad was gone more than he was home, but when he did come home he always had presents for my sister and me. One sunny June afternoon a few days before school was out for the summer, Dad arrived carrying a large white bag. Lyn and I rushed to the door.

"I got you girls a present!" he exclaimed, walking into the living room.

"What did you get us this time, Daddy?" I asked, bouncing on my toes and wiggling with anticipation.

He pulled out a paper bucket.

"Suckers!" I shouted, seeing brightly colored candy lollipops piled right up to the brim.

Just then Mom walked in. When she saw the bucket, she stopped and glared at Dad. "Why did you get the girls so much candy?" she said. "I just had them at the dentist. We can't afford to pay for more cavities."

In an instant, Dad's face flushed beet red. Without a word he opened the front door and threw the bucket as hard as he could out into the front yard. Red, orange, green and yellow lollipops flew through the air and scattered everywhere in the grass.

I was frozen, my excitement replaced with fear. My throat stung like I had just swallowed a swarm of bees.

"God dammit, Joan!" Dad shouted. "I was just trying to make my girls happy!" He slammed the screen door and stormed into his bedroom.

Mom stood silent. Lyn and I ran over to her, crying. She gently placed her arms around us. I couldn't understand why Daddy would throw our lollipops all over the yard. I had been so happy to see him.

THE FIRST WEEK OF summer vacation, Mom loaded Lyn and me into her Ford Fairlane and drove us to meet her family in

Fort Lauderdale, Florida. I knew I had cousins and aunts and uncles on my mom's side, but I had never met them.

Mile after mile, she stared ahead at the road, breaking the silence every once in a while to tell us more about her family. Her mom and dad came from Sweden, she told us, and she was born in Cleveland, Ohio, in 1931, early in the Great Depression. She had two older brothers and a sister—my uncles and aunt. She and her mom moved to Florida when she was eighteen. She told us that she met our dad in Jacksonville a year later. He had moved from Atlanta to Florida to sell aluminum home siding in his father's company, with our grandpa, Bert Rosenthal.

While Mom talked, Lyn and I sipped Coca-Colas and ate peanut butter and jelly sandwiches that she had packed for us to take on the trip. I tried to imagine our mom's Swedish family that I had never met. It was kind of hard to believe that my mom was ever a kid like me.

"When I was little, we were poor," she said, "so we moved to the country where we could grow our own food and have chickens. I had a wonderful childhood running around on that farm, picking wild flowers. My father built me a rope swing in a big oak tree in our yard. I was born eight years after my sister, so I was the baby of the family and my dad doted on me. I was his baby girl and he adored me. I loved him so much," she said.

I put my sandwich in my lap.

"Grandpa died, didn't he, Mom?" I asked.

It took her a moment to reply. "Yes. He died when I was nine."

She sounded as if she were talking to herself. "It was just a minor surgery," she said, "to help get rid of an infection he got from blisters on his feet. I remember when the phone rang on the second day he was in the hospital. My mother screamed and collapsed with the receiver clutched in her hand. A blood clot had gone to his heart.

"I didn't really understand what death was, but I understood quickly that Daddy was gone, that he was never coming back. I missed him so much. I was sad for years. I so wish you girls could have met him. He was only forty-eight years old when he died."

She stopped. A moment later she took a deep breath and looked at us in the rearview mirror. "It's a sad story, girls. I know. I'm sorry," she said.

Lyn and I sat quietly in the back seat. I thought about our own dad. I didn't like it when he got mad, but I sure would hate it if I didn't have a daddy anymore.

"Most families were recovering from the Depression," Mom said after a bit, "but because my dad died, we were terribly poor. Us kids had to take care of things because our mother just fell apart after Dad's death. She didn't leave the house for two years. Finally, after the war started, she got a job for a while in a munitions factory. It was just Mom and me at home by then, but the others helped as best they could. Around the end of the war I dropped out of high school and went to work to support us. I was only fourteen. That's why I keep telling you girls to do well in school, so you can go to college someday. You need to be able to get good jobs so you can take care of yourselves."

We spent five days at my aunt and uncle's house, playing with my cousins. I remember that trip not only because I met my mom's side of the family, but also because Mom agreed to let Lyn and me bring home my aunt and uncle's German schnauzer, Pierre. They'd named him Pierre because they thought he was a poodle. For some reason they wanted to get rid of him, so on the last day of our visit we packed Pierre in our car along with our suitcases and drove away.

When we lived on Alverado Way, we had two cats, Mittens and Mr. Ming, a mynah bird named Joe that talked, multiple goldfish that we buried in Hershey candy wrappers in the yard when they died, white mice with red eyes, and yellow peep chicks at Easter time. But Pierre was the best pet we ever had.

Mom let me sleep with Pierre in my bed at night. He followed me around the neighborhood while I rode my two-wheeler, and he danced with me even though I could tell he didn't like it much. I would hold his front paws at my waist while he struggled to hop along on his two hind legs.

"That's it, Pierre. One, two, cha-cha-cha," I coaxed him as we moved slowly around the living room.

The summer of 1962 was coming to an end; soon we would be back in school. But first our daddy was taking us out to eat to celebrate my sister's tenth birthday.

Dad loved taking us out to restaurants. I loved it too. When he took us to the Waffle House, I always got the grilled cheese that they made in the waffle iron. I would nibble at the delicious little crusty squares and scoop up the melted cheese that oozed out the sides. Sometimes he took us downtown to Caruso's Italian Restaurant. He would help me tie on the bib that I wore along with everyone else, even the adults, so we wouldn't get red sauce on our clothes, and would hold a long piece of spaghetti high over my head with a fork. I'd grab the end with my tongue and suck it into my mouth, sauce splattering over my face. We'd all laugh except for Mom. As I recall, in those days our mom didn't smile or laugh much.

I couldn't wait to see where Dad was taking us this time. I raced into my room and found my sister already there, picking out her outfit.

"You can't wear that!" she said when I pulled a wrinkled Mickey Mouse sweatshirt over my head.

I did my best to ignore her.

"Daddy's taking us out to a restaurant. You have to wear a dress," she said.

"But I don't want to wear a dress," I protested. Poking my head out in the hall I shouted, "Mommy, do I have to wear a dress?"

I could hear my mother's distant voice from her bedroom.

"Yes, Sweetie. Let Lyn help you. I'm still getting ready."

I felt miffed that my sister was right, but then she was always right when it came to outfits. I would set off for school in the morning in my scuffed-up red Keds and pedal pushers, while Lyn would be all spiffed up in her blue plastic pop-bead necklace that matched her pastel blue chiffon dress, which was fluffed out with stiff, crackly petticoats underneath.

Now my fashion-plate big sister smiled smugly as she reached into our small closet and wrestled out a dress identical

Mom with Lyn and me wearing the velvet dresses our grandma made for us.

to the one she had on. Most of our dresses were made by our grandma Margaret, our dad's mom, who lived in Doraville, Georgia, just about thirty minutes from our house in Decatur.

Our grandma used to say that my sister and I were close enough in age to be twins. She would sit in her small, cluttered sewing room on Alison Drive, blowing Tareyton cigarette smoke out her mouth and inhaling it through her nose while she whipped out pairs of dresses from the same pattern. When she wasn't puffing on a cigarette, she would use her mouth to hold all the straight pins that she picked out of the material when she sewed up a seam. For Christmas, I might end up with a burgundy crushed-velvet dress and Lyn a baby blue.

I heard Daddy's voice in the hallway as I jacked my leg up on the edge of my bed and tried to fasten the strap on the black patent-leather shoes my sister told me I had to wear.

"Hey, dolls, are you ready to go to the restaurant? You look so pretty."

I glanced up to see his smiling face in the doorway.

"Where are we going to eat?" I asked.

"Your favorite. Morrison's Cafeteria."

"Oh, boy!" I giggled back at my daddy. I pictured the piece of coconut cream pie I would slide across the silver counter onto my plastic tray.

My mom's high heels clicked on the wooden floor of the hallway as she passed my room.

"It's time to go," Dad said. "I'll meet you in the living room."

But when my sister and I walked out to the living room, a perfectly matched pair, Mom and Dad were already outside. Dad's voice carried right through the door. I stopped and looked at Lyn to see what she was going to do.

Just then Pierre trotted over to us. I leaned down and gently patted his head. For a brief moment I forgot about my daddy's loud voice. "You can go with us next time," I told him. He walked back to his spot next to the couch and lay down.

Lyn inched up to the front door with me close behind. She pushed her thumb on the stubborn, slightly rusted latch of our screen door until it bent back. The door swung open. Our dad had yelled at our mom lots of times. Maybe if he saw us he would stop. We walked out onto the porch.

"Dammit, Joan!" Dad shouted. "I told you I'll have the money next week!"

They were down in the yard just off to the right of the porch, in front of the sticker bushes that lined the picture windows in our living room. They didn't even glance over at us.

My father's face was bright red. Tears rolled down my mother's cheeks and made wet spots on her beige taffeta blouse. I felt like my feet were stuck to the porch with Elmer's Glue. Lyn stood next to me, as still as I was.

"Did you hear me, Joan? Get off my back," Dad blurted at Mom, spit spraying from his mouth.

"Harold, I can't take this anymore!" Mom yelled at him. Her mouth tightened. She raised her arms, put her hands on my father's chest and shoved him.

Caught off guard, Dad lost his balance and fell into the row of sticker bushes, which were covered with spiny thorns. He reared up instantly, his fists tightly clenched.

I opened my mouth to yell "Stop," but nothing came out.

With a quick, hard jab and a blunt undercut, our father punched our mother in the face. She slumped to her knees on the grass. Dad dropped his arms to his sides and stepped back.

I could hardly see through the tears in my eyes. I didn't want to see. I was terrified.

"Mommy!" I screamed, leaping off the top step and running in front of Daddy. I threw my arms around her shoulders and buried my face in her body, sobbing so hard that I could barely breathe. She was trembling.

I dimly heard Daddy's voice. "Lyn, go in the house and bring me a towel for your mother."

Moments later I peered back toward the porch and saw Lyn holding out the towel. Her hands were shaking. Dad reached over, wrapped the towel around Mom's face and helped her stand up. I shivered, shifting from one foot to the other next to Mom and Dad in the chill of dusk. I watched as Dad took our mom by her arm and helped her up the porch steps. Lyn and I followed them back into the darkening living room.

Dad clicked the switch on the gold pole lamp near the front door and pulled back the towel that was covering Mom's face. I saw red spots on it.

"Girls, get in the car," he said. "We're taking your mom to the hospital."

We slid into the back seat of the car without saying a word. We were supposed to be a happy family driving to Morrison's Cafeteria. Instead we were headed for DeKalb General Hospital. While the doctors helped our mom, Lyn and I sat on hard plastic chairs, looking for the hidden broomstick, mouse and ice skate in a *Highlights* magazine we found on the waiting room floor.

At last Dad pushed open the shiny metal emergency room doors and came out with Mom holding his arm. She had white gauze wrapped around her face, like one of the mummies my third-grade teacher, Mrs. Anderson, had shown us in *National Geographic*. I looked away.

We walked to the car in silence. I didn't feel afraid anymore, but all the way home I tried and failed to swallow the big hot lump in my throat. When we opened the front door, Pierre bounded up to me. I kneeled to hug his furry neck.

My whole body softened. Holding him in my arms helped me feel like things were a little bit more normal.

The cuts on Mom's face healed, her stitches were removed and her bruises faded, but things in the house changed after our dad hit our mom. When he was around, she rarely spoke to him. I spent more time outside playing when he was in the house. I didn't know when his mood would change. I didn't know when he would yell at Mommy or maybe hit her again.

FOURTH GRADE STARTED. We had a new routine. Mom started working part-time. She told us that she needed to work to help pay the bills.

One cool autumn evening after we'd done our homework, my sister and I were wading in the nearby creek, chasing water spiders, when we heard Mom's familiar call.

"Lyn, Jeri! Supper's ready!"

She always had to call us a few times before we would stop what we were doing and race each other to the house, wash our hands in the kitchen sink and sit down at the dinner table.

That night, as usual, Dad was out of town working. Mom talked more at dinnertime when Dad was gone, and this time, as I was scooping a steaming spoonful of macaroni and cheese into my mouth, Mom smiled and said, "Hey, how would you girls like to take horseback riding lessons together?"

She knew how much I liked horses. I collected horse figurines, colored yellow manes and brown tails in my stack of horse coloring books and told her about how I dreamed of horses at night. My sister and I were saving up our allowance in Penelope, a ceramic pink piggy bank, to buy our very own horse one day.

I swallowed quickly. "I would love to do that, Mom!"

"Me too!" Lyn exclaimed.

Two weeks later the three of us went to Vogt's Riding Academy. When we got out of the car, no one was around. It was quiet and still except for a breeze that tossed fallen leaves around on the hard-packed dirt where we stood. Then I heard the faint neighing of a horse from inside the barn-like wooden structure in front of us. My stomach fluttered. I had been living for this moment ever since Mom had said we could take riding lessons.

Lyn and I followed Mom inside the barn. The warm smells of hay and horse engulfed me as my eyes adjusted to the dimness. A woman's boisterous voice cut through the still air. I jumped.

"Hello. Hello. Come in! I'm Teresa Vogt," the voice shouted. Then I saw her, a small round woman with short white hair standing next to the biggest horse I had ever seen. She looked straight at me and motioned me over to her.

"Come here, child!" she said. "This is Zastro, the horse you'll be riding."

My legs wobbled. I held my breath and walked toward her. I was stupefied by Zastro's size and beauty. I wanted to reach out and touch him, but I was too afraid.

Teresa told me to lift my left leg. She cupped her muscular hands under my foot and threw me up in the air. I landed with a thud squarely in the English saddle on Zastro's back. My breath whooshed out of me.

"Here. Take the reins like this, one in each hand," Teresa barked in her thick German accent. She wrapped a leather strap around and around to make the stirrups short enough for my nine-year-old legs.

"Go ahead and start walking Zastro around the barn while I help your mom and sister," Teresa told me. I didn't budge. I was petrified. I had never been that high off the ground on a living creature.

"Go ahead! Push him with your legs and dig in with your heels," Teresa shouted up at me.

I leaned just a tiny bit forward in the saddle, and to my amazement and utter delight I felt Zastro's gigantic body shift under me. Hope and determination flickered through my otherwise stiff and nervous body as he lifted one leg, then another, and plodded to the end of the barn. And stopped. I pulled the left rein slightly and he shifted to the left. Could I be controlling this huge animal? I felt about the size of the flies that Zastro swatted off his back with one flick of his tail, but I pulled the rein a bit more and he turned; I shuddered with excitement as, together, we swayed back to where we had started.

After that, weekdays could not pass fast enough. I longed for the moment on Saturday when our car turned onto the long gravel driveway of Vogt's Riding Academy. Mom and Lyn quit riding after a couple of sessions, but not me. I was hooked on the horses and roused by the challenge of learning proper English riding techniques, like posting when a horse trots. Mom bought me a velvet hunt cap, riding boots and, my favorite part of the outfit, jodhpurs.

Me and my sister in front of our house.

When Teresa asked me to stay after lessons to help feed the horses, I spent precious private time alone with Alco, Flora, Zelda and Zastro, stroking their soft, warm shoulders and running my fingers through their manes. I was in love with these magical animals; they captivated me with their massive bodies and their big, expressive eyes.

In between Saturdays, I worked on my riding posture in front of the full-length mirror that hung on the back of my mom's bedroom door. When Dad was home, I recruited him to trot around the front yard with me on his back to help strengthen my leg muscles. He not only trotted but galloped and bucked while I squeezed his waist as hard as I could to keep from falling off.

After four months of lessons, I competed in my first dressage horse show and won a third-place ribbon that I proudly tacked up on my bedroom wall.

"Someday soon, Jeri, you'll be ready to start jumping," Teresa told me, squeezing my shoulder with her strong grip.

A MONTH OR SO AFTER the horse show, Dad told Lyn and me that he was going to take us somewhere really special. He had a big surprise for us.

"Where are we going, Daddy?" I asked, half running, half skipping behind him and Lyn to the car.

"Harold, where are you taking the girls?"

I stopped and turned around to see Mom standing on the front porch with her hands on her hips. I held my breath. Was she going to tell Dad not to take us? I looked from her to him and back again.

"Somewhere," Dad replied without looking at her. His eyes locked with mine. Smiling, he said, "Let's go, girls! I have something to show you that you're going to like."

I slid into the back seat next to Lyn. As we drove away, I turned around in my seat and watched through the rear window as Mom dropped her arms, turned and went alone inside the house. I wondered why she couldn't come with us. I really wanted her to come, but I didn't say anything to Dad. Instead I tried to think more about the surprise he had waiting for us.

It was a long drive.

About an hour after we left our house, the landscape changed from densely packed pine trees to fields of corn and pastures with cows and some horses.

"Daddy, where are we?" I asked.

"We're out in the country," he said. Ten minutes later he parked in front of a small white house and turned off the ignition. He jumped out of the car and opened our door.

"I got you girls a farm!" he exclaimed, his eyes bright.

"You got us a real live farm, Daddy?" I asked, scrambling out of the back seat as fast as I could.

"That's right," he replied. He grabbed my hand and walked me on one side of him and Lyn on the other toward a worn wooden structure that looked like a barn.

"What animals do we have on our farm, Daddy?" I asked.

He stopped and pointed. "There!"

A white horse with large black and brown spots stood in a fenced area next to the barn.

"I bought you a horse!" he said gleefully.

"Daddy, oh, Daddy! A horse. You got us a horse!" I squealed.

I wanted to race over to the animal, but I knew from my lessons that fast movements spook horses. As slowly as I could, I walked over to get a better look.

Lyn stood next to me, staring through the slats in the fence. "Can we go inside, Dad?" she asked.

"Sure you can," he said.

We followed him inside the corral and cautiously went up to the horse. He didn't move away from us. I fluttered with excitement. Having my *own* horse was better than riding horses at the academy. They didn't belong to just me. I reached out and touched his mane. He stood still.

I beamed back at my dad. "I think he likes me!"

"I'm sure he does," Dad said, smiling.

"Can we ride him, Daddy?" Lyn asked.

Dad put his arms around our shoulders and pulled us in tight, saying, "Does your daddy make you happy?"

Lyn and I answered together, "Yes, Daddy!"

"There's a saddle inside the barn," he said.

We followed him to the barn door. I held my breath while he fumbled with the latch. I couldn't wait to see what was inside. Chickens or goats, I imagined. Maybe kittens.

As the door swung open, the smell of gasoline and grease wafted out. I stood and stared, no chickens, goats or kittens in sight. That barn was full of cars.

I was bewildered. "Dad, where are all the cows and chickens?" I asked.

A big man in a blue, grease-stained jumpsuit stepped out from the shadow of an open car hood with some sort of tool in his hand. I recognized him from a junkyard our dad had taken me to a few weeks earlier.

"Hey, Harold," the man said.

"Billy, you remember my girls, Lyn and Jeri."

"Well, yes. I remember your girls, Harold," he said, staring at us.

I moved closer to Daddy and stayed right next to him until he grabbed the saddle and we emerged into the sunlight. I was relieved to get away from the smelly barn, the grease-stained man and all those cars.

Me and Lyn riding Mickey bareback at the farm.

A different man helped us secure the saddle on our horse. I helped too. Teresa had shown me how to cinch a saddle and put on a bridle. Lyn wanted to go first, so I sat on the fence while she rode around the corral.

I could hardly sit still waiting for my turn. Finally Lyn dismounted. I walked up to our horse and stroked his thick white mane. He had a chocolate-brown face with a wide white stripe down the middle. He was the most beautiful horse I had ever seen!

Once on his back, I held the reins as I had learned in my riding lessons and tried to control his gait by squeezing my legs. He seemed to respond, walking easily around the corral and then out to the grassy meadow. I guided him alongside a stream toward a distant line of pine trees. It didn't seem to me that we had been gone long when I heard Lyn calling me.

Reluctantly, I pulled on the reins and turned around. Lyn was perched on the corral fence, waving at me.

In the car going home, Lyn and I decided to name our new horse Mickey after Mickey Mouse. We sang the Mickey Mouse song over and over again, swapping out the word "mouse" with "horse." "H-O-R-S-E," we sang in unison. I couldn't wait to tell Mom about Mickey, but when I did she only smiled for a minute and told me that I had to finish my homework.

Several days passed without Dad mentioning the farm. I finally asked, "Dad, when can we go back out to the farm and see Mickey?"

"Soon, Pumpkin," he said.

But soon wasn't soon enough. Day after day, week after week, I waited. A whole month went by. I worried that Mickey was hungry or lonely without me there to take care of him. But I was mostly worried that he wouldn't remember me.

ONE DAY WHEN LYN and I got home from school, our dad's car was in the driveway. I rushed into the house, hoping that he was going to take me out to see Mickey, but when we went inside, our mom and dad were sitting together on the couch, which they never did. Mom looked like she had been crying. I stopped in my tracks.

As soon as he saw us, Dad got up. He walked over to us, kneeled down and put his arms around our waists. Tears welled in his eyes. "Pierre was hit by a car this morning. He didn't make it. He died."

I burst into tears and fell onto Dad's shoulder, sobbing. I heard Lyn crying too.

Dad held us for a long time. Then he took us out for ice cream. When we got home, Lyn and I leaned out our bedroom window and watched through our tears as Dad dug a hole to bury Pierre, who lay on the grass, wrapped in a sheet. Once the hole was deep enough, Dad placed Pierre's body inside and shoveled dirt on top until my best friend disappeared under a mound of Georgia red clay.

Everything changed for me after Pierre died. Looking back, I see that Pierre's death began a startling sequence of events that would shatter the foundation of everything I trusted and believed would stay the same. Up until then I had my dog, my sister, my mom and dad, my house, school, neighborhood and friends. I was rooted in a belief that the most important things in my life would always be there.

THREE DAYS LATER, Lyn and I were sitting in front of the TV, watching Sunday morning cartoons and eating Cheerios, when Dad came into the living room. "Okay, girls," he exclaimed. "We're going out to the farm today."

I rushed to my room to get ready. At last I was going to get to see Mickey.

Mom didn't come with us, and this time she didn't ask where we were going, or stand on the porch as we drove away. She stayed busy in the kitchen.

And Dad made a stop on the way out of town.

"We're picking up my secretary," he said, not offering any further explanation as he pulled up outside a redbrick apartment building with green-and-white-striped awnings.

We waited in the back seat while Dad went to get this secretary, whoever she was. He came out with a woman in a tight black skirt and knee-high patent-leather boots. She didn't look like she was going to a farm. Dad opened the passenger door for her. She bent over and ducked into the car to keep from messing up her blonde beehive.

When Dad got behind the wheel he turned, looked back at us and said, "Lyn, Jeri, this is Joyce."

"Hey, girls. Nice to meet y'all. Your daddy has told me a lot about you," she said.

I stared out the window and quietly said, "Hello." I wished we were at the farm already so I could see if Mickey was all right.

As soon as Dad pulled into the driveway, I threw open the car door and saw our horse standing in the corral.

"Mickey!" I shouted, waving my arm. When he tossed his head up and neighed, I knew that he recognized me. "I'm coming, Mickey!" I sang out.

After I gave him a few kisses on his face and several strokes down his long, soft neck, Dad helped us, as he had before, get the saddle from the barn.

It was my turn to go first. I climbed up on the fence, swung my leg out and landed on Mickey's back. Lyn walked with Joyce back up to the house. Dad was inside the barn talking to Billy. I reined Mickey to head out to the meadow.

We had gone no more than a few yards when he turned around and trotted back to the corral. I pulled on the reins to tell him to stop, but he ignored me. When we got to the corral, I turned him once again and kicked him with my heels. At first he went out as he had done before, but again he turned around on his own and trotted back. Why was he ignoring me? The horses at the academy never did that.

Frustrated, I called out, "Dad!"

He squinted in the bright sunlight as he emerged from the barn and shouted something over his shoulder to Billy before he walked toward me.

"Mickey won't mind me," I said, certain my daddy could help. "He won't go out to the meadow. He keeps trotting back to the corral. Can you walk us farther out? I think that will help him keep going."

Without looking up at me, Dad took Mickey by the bridle and walked with us down the gravel driveway.

His silence made me feel like I had disrupted him. Not wanting to bother him, I said, "This is far enough, Dad."

He let go of the bridle and watched as Mickey turned around and trotted back to the corral with me bouncing up and down on his back shouting, "Whoa, Mickey! Stop, Mickey!"

I had my back to Dad, so I had no warning when he appeared next to us, his face pinched and red. He grabbed Mickey's bridle and jerked hard as he yelled, "God dammit! I'm going to teach this horse a lesson!"

He reached up and yanked me off Mickey's back. "Run into the house, Jeri!" he said.

My heart leapt into my throat. For a moment I stopped breathing. I saw the whites of Mickey's eyes as he threw his head up and tried to get away from my dad.

I turned and ran as fast as I could. Panting for breath, I scrambled onto the porch where Joyce and Lyn were standing. They must have heard Dad yelling and come out. They stared past me as I ran to them. I didn't see what they saw: Dad pulling Mickey into the barn and coming out again with a rifle in his hand, still dragging my horse.

"Come here, girls!" Joyce yelled, motioning us inside. She slammed the door shut and pushed a coffee table onto its side. "Duck behind here!" she told us, her voice shrill.

Shaking, I darted across the room and knelt behind the table next to Lyn.

When I heard Dad shouting, "You Goddamn son-of-a-bitch horse," I peered over the table and out the window. He had Mickey by the reins, pulling him as Mickey jerked away. Dad swung the rifle up in the air.

"He's going to shoot Mickey!" I screamed.

As if it were happening in slow motion, I watched Dad let go of the reins, put both hands on the rifle and swing it like a baseball bat, hitting Mickey in the neck. Mickey reared and bolted down the driveway toward the road. I slumped behind the table, crying.

Minutes later I heard the front door open. I dragged myself to my feet and stared at Dad, who stood in the doorway, the rifle hanging by his side.

"Why are you behind that table?" he asked calmly.

I couldn't speak or move. In my mind I saw myself running over to him, kicking and hitting him as hard as I could, but there I stood, frozen. Dad motioned us to follow him out the door, saying with a half-hearted smile, "Lyn, Jeri, let's go find your horse. It's going to be okay."

We got in the car and drove along back roads, past neighboring farms. I rolled down my window and shouted "Mickey!" over and over. But after a good hour of looking, we didn't find him.

Riding home, I cowered in the back seat, not saying a word as the sky got darker and darker. I felt like someone had punched me in the stomach and knocked all the wind out of me. I couldn't wait to get away from my dad. I couldn't wait to return to my mommy's arms.

3

Mommy's Not Here

The house was pitch black when we pulled into the driveway. I opened our front door and rushed inside.

"Mommy! We're home," I shouted, flicking on the hall light and racing into her room.

There was no answer.

"Mommy, we're home," Lyn echoed behind me.

By now Dad was inside. I ran back to the living room.

"Where's Mommy?" I asked, frantic.

"Joan. Joan, are you here?" Dad called.

Still no answer.

"Mommy's not here," I said as warm tears rolled out of my eyes.

"Well, girls, don't worry. I'll call her friend Sylvia and see if she's over there. Get into your pajamas."

I darted into my bedroom, clinging to a shred of hope that if I got my pajamas on as I did every night, Mom would appear, and Mickey would be okay too. I found my pajamas in my dresser drawer.

Dad was just hanging up the phone when Lyn and I, both dressed for bed, walked into his room.

"She's there," he said, "at Sylvia's. She told me to get you girls to bed. She's spending the night over there and she'll come home after work tomorrow."

Mom had never spent the night away from us before.

Dad tucked us in and kissed us good night.

"They found Mickey on a neighbor's farm," he said when he turned out the light.

As soon as the door was closed, I rolled over in my bed and cried. I wanted to believe that he was telling the truth about my horse, but I wasn't sure.

It never crossed my mind that he might be lying to me about our mom.

THE NEXT DAY I walked home from school with my sister as usual. I pulled open the screen door, my heart filled with hope, and in my hand a piece of yellow construction paper with a drawing I had made for Mom.

"Mom," I called. "Mom!"

The house was empty.

Just then I heard a car in the driveway. I raced out the front door with Lyn right beside me. *Maybe it's Mommy*, I thought, but it was my dad.

"Daddy, Daddy, Daddy, where's Mom?" I shouted as he came around the front of the car.

"Come here, girls. Your mom is visiting her sister in Florida," he said calmly. He clutched me and put his head next to mine. When I looked up at him, he pushed my bangs across my forehead.

I couldn't make sense of what was happening. Why would Mommy leave me? Why wouldn't she take me with her to Florida? Why didn't she tell me where she was going? These thoughts ran through my mind as I stood there, shaking and silent, in my daddy's arms.

THE TRUTH WAS THAT Dad had no idea where Mom was, when she would be back or even if she would ever return. While we were at the farm that Sunday, April 14, 1963, our mom had packed a suitcase, got in her car and started driving. She had thirty-five dollars in her wallet. She drove for days. When she got to Arizona, her 1960 green Ford Fairlane broke down in the desert, and she didn't have the money to fix it. She called a friend who wired her two hundred dollars. She got her car repaired and drove to Los Angeles, which was as far from our father as she could go. Mom was all alone in one of the biggest cities in the United States.

I didn't understand until much later why our mother left us without saying goodbye, or why she would leave us at all. When I was around thirteen, Mom told me what it was like living with our father on Alverado Way and why she ran all the way across the country to get away from him.

She explained that because her father died when she was a child, she thought it was her duty to keep our family together, even though Dad abused her. She didn't want us to feel the loss she had felt when her dad died.

But she reached a breaking point. When her father was alive, her parents were affectionate and sweet to one another. She thought her marriage would be like that too, and it was at first. She and Dad were nineteen when they met and only twenty-one in 1952 when Lyn was born. Fourteen months later, in October 1953, I was born. But after we had been living on Alverado Way for a couple of years, things changed. Dad started saying mean, degrading things to Mom and yelling at her. She was terrified of him, so she never argued with him. This went on for a year or so until that day he hit her in front of us. I was shocked to learn that he told Mom he would kill her if she ever took us away from him. "That's why I left without you," she said to me.

In the early sixties, unlike today, domestic violence was never mentioned in magazines or discussed on talk shows. When it happened, it was a secret. While laws against it existed, the police and the criminal justice system considered domestic violence to be a family problem, a private matter rather than a crime.

Women like my mother were on their own. There were no shelters or programs. The first shelters and crisis hotlines for battered women in the United States were set up in the 1970s. My mother was a victim of domestic violence before it even had a name.

The second day without Mom passed, and then a third. On the fourth day I waited for the school bell to ring so I could race home to see if she was back. As always, I met up with my sister at the flagpole to walk home.

"I bet Mom's home when we get there," I said, walking a little faster.

"I bet she's not," Lyn said.

"When do you think she'll be home?" I asked. "She can't stay that long in Florida, especially without us."

Lyn paused for a moment as if she were thinking about it.

"Saturday. She'll be home on Saturday. I'll race you!" she said, taking off down the street. I ran as fast as I could after her. When I got within sight of our house, Lyn was already at the front door.

"Wait for me!" I shouted, but she didn't. She disappeared inside.

Seconds later I burst into the living room and shouted, "Mom! Mom! Are you here?"

There was no answer.

That night when it was dark and quiet, I lay in my bed trying to hold Mom in my mind as I fell asleep. I wanted her back so she could sit next to me and listen to me read from one of my library books. I wanted her to give me a quarter so I could sprint across the yard to buy a Popsicle from the ice-cream truck. I wanted to hear her calling me in for supper. Even though my sister was sleeping in the bed right next to me, without my mom in the house I felt completely alone.

Mom didn't come home on Saturday as Lyn had said she would. I didn't really believe her anyway. Instead of Mom coming home that day, Dad took Lyn and me to get Krystal hamburgers and told us that we were going to spend a few days at our grandma's house.

"What about school, Dad?" I asked.

"Oh, it's okay if you miss a couple of days," he said.

"Why can't we stay at our house?" I asked, so quietly it was almost a whisper.

"You just can't right now," he said in a loud voice that made me jump.

Two hours later, Dad put my suitcase in the trunk of the car along with Lyn's and slammed it shut. Lyn and I sat silently in the back seat with our Barbie dolls between us in a cardboard box. Dad reversed the car out of our driveway and drove up Alverado Way. I got on my knees and peered out the back window, seeing our house get smaller and smaller. As we crested the hill, it dropped out of sight. The tear that fell from my cheek onto the car upholstery left a dark, wet spot. It was soon joined by another.

I never returned to our house on Alverado Way. I never took another piano lesson from Mrs. Montgomery or learned how to jump horses at Vogt's Riding Academy.

"I have to work out of town," Dad said when he dropped us off at our grandma's house. He kissed us goodbye and pulled out of the driveway. I had been at Grandma's many times, but this was the first time I was going to spend the night. I wanted to tell my dad to stay with me, but I couldn't get the words out. Instead I watched him drive away down the street.

"Girls, you'll be sleeping in my room," Grandma said, kneeling down and putting her arms around us. "Now go brush your teeth and get into your pajamas."

After we said our prayers and got under the covers, I summoned my courage and asked my grandma, "When is our mom coming home?"

She reached over and stubbed out her cigarette in the ashtray on her nightstand, looked back at me and said, "Your mother has a drinking problem. She's getting help."

"I thought she was visiting her sister in Florida," Lyn said.

The wrinkles on Grandma's forehead raised up closer to her gray bangs. "Well," she said, "she did visit her sister, but she had to leave to get help for her drinking."

"When is she coming home?" I asked again.

"Well, I'm not sure, Jeri," she responded.

My eyes filled with tears.

She looked at me, reached over and patted my shoulder. "I'm sure she won't be gone long," she told us. "It's time for you to go to sleep now." She turned from me and stared at the flickering images on the portable black-and-white TV that stood on the chest of drawers across from the bed.

I rolled over, away from the TV's glare. I couldn't sleep. I couldn't stop thinking about what Grandma said. My mom had a drinking problem. I wished she would get better soon and come home. I tossed over onto my stomach and cried softly into my pillow so Grandma couldn't hear me.

Looking back, I realize our mom didn't have a drinking problem. I never found out why our grandma said that.

Our grandma.

Maybe Dad told Grandma that Mom had a drinking problem in order to explain why she left. Or Grandma could just as well have made it up to have something to tell us, to explain why our mom disappeared.

INSTEAD OF GOING TO school the next day, Lyn and I helped Grandma plant marigolds in her backyard. When we sat down to eat dinner that night, Grandpa was already at the table, pouring himself a drink of whisky. He held up his glass and slurred, "These are the folks, jokes," laughing about turning the words around. Even at ten I knew it was supposed to be "these are the jokes, folks."

I figured our grandma knew what a drinking problem was because our grandpa drank every night until he passed out. One time his cigar fell out of his mouth and lit the sofa on fire.

I never saw Mom act like my grandpa. I saw her drinking at parties we sometimes had at our house, but she never slurred her words or fell over. I couldn't understand why she would leave me unless she was getting help, unless she needed something I couldn't give her.

After a week, Grandma told us that we were going to enroll at Northwoods Elementary School a few blocks from her house. I would continue in fourth grade and Lyn in fifth for the next month until we were out for summer vacation.

I was getting used to living with my grandparents. Lyn and I played with the Womack girls down the street, and our grandma was most always in a good mood, laughing, cooking and teaching my sister and me things like how to properly set the table and bake Welsh cookies.

Now I realize that our grandma stepped in to raise my sister and me when our parents couldn't. She really was the only grandparent I had who was capable of taking care of us. My mom's father died before I was born, and Mom's mom was sick and lived far away in Florida. My dad's father, Grandpa Bert, was an alcoholic. I had little interaction with him during my life, even when I lived there with them as a child. He frightened me.

My sister and I lived with our grandparents just like so many children do today due to the epidemic of drug addiction, mass incarceration and domestic violence. It didn't occur to me until recently that back then in the 1960s we were a statistic and didn't even know it. Today, in 2019, more than seven million American grandparents are raising their grandchildren.

WHILE LYN AND I were settling into our new routine, Mom was renting the cheapest apartment she could find in Los Angeles and was working in a pathology lab, a job she landed the first week she arrived in California. She borrowed money from her boss to get her through until her first paycheck. Her car broke down again, so every day she would get up and take the bus downtown to work.

Years later when I asked her how it was for her, leaving Lyn and me and living so far away from Georgia, she said, "That was the most frightening time in my life. I missed you girls so much. I used to sing a song to myself every day to try to feel better. It was 'Smile.' Nat King Cole's version. Do you know that song?"

I nodded and she went on to recite a few lines: "*Smile, though your heart is aching, Smile, even though it's breaking, When there are clouds in the sky, you'll get by.*"

"One afternoon when I was riding the bus home from work," she told me, "a group of kids got on and started singing 'Puff the Magic Dragon,' you girls' favorite song. I broke down in tears. I couldn't stand being away from you two girls. No matter how afraid I was of your dad, I had to go back to you."

Our mother quit her job and bought a one-way bus ticket back to Atlanta. She had been gone for six months. When Dad picked her up at the bus station, he called to tell us that our mother would be at my grandma's in less than an hour. I remember I was so excited I couldn't eat the scrambled eggs and toast our grandma had made for us.

"Jeri, you need to eat something," Grandma told me as I sat staring at my plate.

"I'm not hungry, Grandma. I can't wait for Mom to get back. When is she going to be here?" I asked, squirming back and forth in my chair.

She tilted her head to one side and smiled. "It won't be long now, girls," she said. "Your mother will be here any time now."

Just then I heard a car door slam shut. I sprang up from the table and flew to the door with Lyn right behind me. Within seconds I was in our mom's arms, tears streaming down my face. I didn't even notice Dad as he got back in the car and drove away. Mom held me and my sister for a long, long time. As we climbed the porch steps together to go inside the house, I held her hand tightly in mine.

Not a word was said by any of us about why she left, where she went or what made her come back.

While we didn't say much back then, Mom, Lyn and I have talked about these times over and over again through the years. Mom told us that talking about troubling times helps heal. But as a child I didn't understand what was happening. It seemed to me that my feelings didn't matter to the people who loved me, because they never asked me how I felt. What I wanted more than anything was not to be left alone and to be assured that I would be taken care of, so I didn't ask many questions. I just followed along with what the adults told me, trying my best to please them.

4

Jailbird

Mom, Lyn and I moved into Peach Valley Apartments shortly after Mom returned. When I asked why Dad wasn't moving in with us, Mom told me that they were separated.

I was so happy to have my mom back, I figured she knew what she needed to do to keep from leaving again. Even though I had been told she left because she had a drinking problem, I suspected that her absence had more to do with how my dad scared her. Now I just wanted everything to be all right. I did my best not to think about the three things I was most afraid of: Mom leaving, Dad getting mad, and having to move again.

Our two-story, redbrick building was the very first one next to the access road. All the buildings in our complex bordered a steep driveway that dropped off into a wooded valley. That's why our apartments were called Peach Valley, even though no peach trees grew there. Georgia was the "Peach State," so pretty much everything was named after peaches.

We didn't have any of the furniture from Alverado Way. The blond lazy Susan table, the three-footed stacking stools and our single beds were all replaced with used-but-new-to-us furniture that Mom bought at Goodwill.

Except for one thing: my piano. Even though I had to stop taking lessons when we left Decatur, I had been studying piano for more than five years by then, and I was playing classical music. Beethoven was my favorite composer. Having my familiar piano in our new home comforted me. I told Mom that I wanted to start taking lessons again, and she agreed, but first she needed to save the money.

"It won't take long," she told me, but it was not to be. Mom was never able to pay for my piano lessons again.

The first night, after we got all of our things more or less settled in our new home, Mom drove us to Winn-Dixie to buy some chicken potpies for what she called a housewarming dinner. When we got to the frozen-food aisle she piled one after another into the buggy until I counted twelve. "They're on sale for a quarter," she explained. She also bought boxes of oatmeal and Rice Krispies, packages of bologna and Wonder Bread, a jar of Miracle Whip and a bottle of milk.

"Okay, girls," she said as we paraded out to the car with two brown paper bags, "we're set all week for breakfast, lunch and dinner."

Even though we were just a couple of exits down the expressway from where my grandparents lived and where I had been going to fourth grade, that September I started fifth grade in a new school, Hawthorne Elementary. Lyn transferred to a new school too, but different from mine.

Nearly everything had changed. Mom was working full-time and spending more weekend nights out. Lyn and I were almost teenagers, with less adult supervision than ever. The apartment was a place to eat, sleep and get ready to go out into the world each day in three different directions. I always breathed a little easier after school when Lyn showed up at the Amoco gas station to walk with me to Grandma's, where we stayed until Mom picked us up. Because we were still in the Northwoods neighborhood where Lyn and I had lived with Grandma, at least I could still hang out with my friends from fifth grade. Cathy was my best friend.

One brisk, bright afternoon about two months after school started, I was waiting for Lyn at the Amoco gas station with a nickel in my pocket that Mom had given me to buy bubble gum. Lyn stepped off the bus just as I gave one hard twist of the handle on the glass-topped vending machine. The cool round blue, orange and red balls dropped into my hand, and I popped two into my mouth. Scurrying over to Lyn, I held out my hand and asked, "Want a gumball?"

"Your hands are dirty," she said with a grimace, but she reached over anyway, took the red one, blew on it to get the germs off and put it in her mouth.

As we walked up Alison Drive where Grandma lived, I saw the 1952 Plymouth we called the Green Hornet parked in the driveway. Mom had bought the Hornet with the horse money Lyn and I had saved in our Penelope piggy bank. She told us that she was just borrowing the money until she could pay us back.

I bounced up the four cement porch stairs, opened the front door and heard muffled voices talking in the living room. When my sister pushed the door shut behind us, the voices stopped. Hearing only the wooden floor creaking beneath my feet, I ran around the corner and into the living room. Mom and Grandma stood up and stared at Lyn and me.

I wanted to race over and hug Mom, but I couldn't. The air felt thick, impenetrable, and I stood motionless just inside the room. It felt to me like the day when Mom and Dad were waiting to tell us that Pierre had died.

"Girls," Mom said with a slight smile, "come over here."

"I thought you were at work," I said as Lyn and I crossed the room toward Grandma's worn orange upholstered chair where Mom had been sitting.

She gripped my shoulder with one hand and Lyn's with the other, and her eyelids fluttered a few times before she said, "Your dad will be gone for a while. He went away to a training school."

My sister was the first one to respond. "I want to tell him goodbye. Where is he?"

"He already left," Mom said, staring past us at the floor.

I glanced over at my sister and watched tears spring to her eyes.

"How long will he be gone?" Lyn asked, her voice shaky.

"A few months," Mom said softly. "He'll call you and write letters. You can write him letters too. The time will pass fast, and he'll be here with you again. Now let's get going. I'm making your favorite, macaroni and cheese." She dropped her arms and reached for her handbag.

I knew Dad would come back. He always came back. I didn't really know why my sister got so upset. After all, he would be back to see us after he finished his training school, and I was sure he would bring us some presents.

Two weeks later, Lyn and I were eating bagels with cream cheese at Grandma's. While our grandpa was Jewish, we never went to a synagogue or were taught anything about the Jewish traditions. Grandma made matzo ball soup every once in a while, but she wasn't Jewish. Most Sundays my sister and I went with our grandma to Northwoods Methodist Church.

"Girls, your dad wrote you a letter," Grandma said, handing the letter to my sister. "Lyn, why don't you read it to us?"

My sister took the lined paper from Grandma's hand and read aloud:

> *November 30, 1963*
> *To my Two-Both.*
>
> *I want to write you both this letter because I sure miss you both more than you will ever know. You sure make me a proud, happy Daddy. I could not ever have done any better than two-both. You guys are funny and happy and this makes me happy. Children are the best part of life, the innocent part that sees things with wonder, the laughter,*

the playfulness, the love. Yes, my girls, I wish I could go back and grow up with you. I tried so hard at times to be as childlike as I could. If only to feel for a moment the total innocence and the complete joy of being like you girls. To know the simplicity of life as seen through your eyes.

I sure do miss you a great big bunch and I love you the most in the whole big, big world. My girls, I am sending you all the love a few words can tell. For only a dad can know the love of girls and I sure know this. Take care of each other and mother and grandmother. I wish I was there with you, but I will be in not too long from now.

From a loving and proud,

Dad

"See, girls. Your daddy loves you," Grandma said.

"Grandma, can I keep the letter?" Lyn asked. "I'll take good care of it."

"Why, of course you can, Lyn," Grandma replied.

SOMETIMES LYN AND I stayed over at our grandma's on Saturday nights when Mom went out with her hairdresser friend, Sylvia. One Sunday morning I was ready for church before Lyn and Grandma, so I decided to look for a piece of satin in my grandma's sewing room.

Ever since I could remember I had rubbed satin, or, as I called it, "silky," with the tips of my fingers. I think I first discovered how wonderful it felt as an infant, when my mom covered me with a blanket trimmed with satin. I never spent the night anywhere without taking silky with me, and to this day I still rub or play with silky to help me fall asleep. Sometimes I think about how much more peaceful this world would be if everyone enjoyed the trance-like calming state that playing with silky gives me.

I rummaged through fabric remnants in a cardboard box that had been pushed underneath an old rickety card table next to my grandma's Singer sewing machine. I glanced up and saw a white envelope sticking out from under a *Life* magazine. I could see the writing on the envelope. It looked like my dad's. I picked it up. It was addressed to my grandma, Margaret Rosenthal. I didn't hear anyone in the hall, so I pulled the letter out, unfolded the lined paper and started reading to myself.

> *Dear Mother,*
>
> *I'm doing Ok. The food is not very good. But I'm making it. Please don't worry about me. Thanks for sending the Welsh cookies. The fellas really liked them. The time will pass fast. Before you know it I will be out of this jail and out there with you and my girls again.*
>
> *Love,*
>
> *Harold*

My eyes fixed on the word "jail." A warm flush spread over my face. Maybe Dad was saying that being at his training school was like being in jail. I stopped reading, folded the letter and slipped it back in the envelope exactly how I found it. When Grandma came out of her bedroom carrying her delicate lace gloves in one hand and her Bible in the other, I was sitting on the couch patting Sugar, her little black lap dog.

Grandma turned and called down the hall. "Lyn, are you ready?"

"Almost," Lyn shouted back.

"Come on, Sweetie. We're going to be late if you don't hurry up."

Grandma saw me sitting on the couch. "Well, I have to say one thing, Jeri. You are always ready on time. Where's your Bible?"

Avoiding her gaze, I looked straight ahead at the large round coffee table in front of me. "Over there," I mumbled. For our Christmas present the year before, Grandma had special-ordered white Bibles for Lyn and me with our names engraved in gold on the front.

As soon as Lyn was ready we walked out into a gray, overcast day. Red leaves from the sweetgum tree in the front yard fluttered across the driveway. When I heard Lyn call "Shotgun," I felt relieved that I didn't have to sit next to Grandma. I slid into the back seat and stared out the window, not saying a word. I was so quiet that Grandma exclaimed, as she turned in to the church parking lot, "Are you all right, Jeri? You sure are quiet back there."

"I'm okay, Grandma," I responded, hoping she couldn't tell from my voice that I was worried that my dad might be in jail. I didn't want to ask her. She might get mad at me for reading her mail.

We followed Grandma into the church and straight up to the first row. I sat down, not taking my eyes off a picture of Jesus hanging on the wall right in front of me. Did Jesus know that I had read my grandma's letter? The organ boomed out "The Old Rugged Cross" as I stood and tried to balance a heavy hymnal in my shaking hands. I couldn't tell anyone about the letter because then they would know I had been a bad girl. And if they knew I had been a bad girl, something terrible would happen.

GROWING UP WITH my sister was like riding side by side on a roller coaster, screaming, but not holding hands or helping each other. We weren't exactly best friends. We did a lot of things together because it was convenient, but sometimes it wasn't convenient at all.

The days grew shorter as winter approached. On a mild afternoon in early December, Lyn and I were outside at Grandma's where the driveway met the black asphalt of Alison Drive. Lyn was hovering over her bicycle, waiting for her best friend, Beth, to come over. They had plans to ride to the shopping center up on Buford Highway to get candy at the five and dime before it got dark.

"You can't come with us," Lyn scoffed at me with an icy, belittling look.

My cheeks burned as they always did when she bossed me around.

"You're a clod. You can't come with us," she repeated.

My heart thumped in my ears. I desperately needed to shut her up. "I know something you don't!" I shouted.

"You don't know anything, you creep," she shot back, spinning her bike away from me and preparing to ride off.

"Dad's in jail. He's a jailbird!" I snapped. I didn't want to believe that Dad was in jail, but in that moment I wanted Lyn to believe he was.

Lyn flipped around. "You're lying!" she shrieked.

"No, I'm not. I saw a letter he wrote to Grandma," I blurted. "I saw it in her sewing room."

Realizing I had told her about the letter, I clapped my hand over my mouth and froze.

Without another word she pushed her bicycle kickstand down and ran past me into the house.

"Where are you going? Don't tell Grandma," I yelled after her, but I knew it was too late.

I had an overwhelming urge to flee but nowhere to go. Before I could figure out what to do next, the porch door opened and Grandma stepped out and looked straight at me. I squirmed under her gaze.

"Jeri, come inside," she said.

I trudged up the porch stairs, through the door she was holding open for me, ducking under her bony, wrinkled arm.

"Let's go to my bedroom and have a talk," she said, pulling the door shut.

When I walked into the bedroom, Lyn was hunched on Grandma's bed, her face wet and red. If only I could take back what I had said. If I hadn't told her that Dad was a jailbird, she wouldn't be sitting there crying like that. And if I hadn't told her that Dad was a jailbird, Grandma wouldn't know I had read her letter. I stood very still except for an uncontrollable quiver that pulsed in my bottom lip.

I waited for Grandma to come in and sit down next to Lyn before I chose a spot at the foot of the bed as far from her as I could get. I clutched the pale blue polyester bedspread and stared at my feet. The bedspread felt stiff and prickly in my sweaty hands. Grandma took a cigarette out of the package on her nightstand and lit it.

"Lyn told me you said that your daddy is in jail. Did you say that?" she asked, puffs of smoke shooting out of her mouth as she spoke.

I swallowed a big ball of fire, and, not looking up from the floor, I nodded.

"She told me that you read a letter in my sewing room. Is that true?"

I nodded again, watching my toes push up and down inside my sneakers like they were trying to escape the tight red canvas.

"Why did you read my letter?" she asked, raising her voice.

That big ball of fire I was trying to hold back burst out with a gush of tears. In between my ragged gulps for air I promised, "I won't do it again, Grandma."

Softening her voice ever so slightly, she said, "You shouldn't read other people's mail. You know better than that, don't you?"

Out of the corner of my eye, I could see her staring at me. A dreadful silence fell. She took drag after drag from her cigarette. I let go of the bedspread long enough to wipe my face with the back of my hands. I looked longingly at the open bedroom door.

Grandma cleared her throat. "Girls," she said, "I have something to tell you about your dad." Her hand, still holding the cigarette, shook. She looked at the floor for a moment, then at Lyn and finally at me. "Your dad is in jail."

Gripping the bedspread once more, I wondered, How could *my* daddy be in jail? I knew that my daddy loved me so much he would never ever go away. How could my daddy, who owned a bail bonding company to help people get out of jail, now be in jail?

I looked at my sister. She was crying so hard her shoulders jerked up and down as she sobbed.

Grandma retrieved a white cotton hankie from her bra and handed it to Lyn. The stinky smoke from her cigarette was suffocating me. I let go of the bedspread and slid to my feet. There was the door, right over there. But Grandma wasn't done.

She cleared her throat. "Jeri, stay here. I have something else to tell you."

I stood still and listened.

"Girls, I don't want you to tell anyone where your dad is. We'll just keep that to ourselves. It'll be our secret. Can you do that?" she asked, tilting her head to one side and staring at me with her gray eyes.

"You don't even need to tell your daddy that you know. Just keep writing him letters like you have been doing," she instructed. "It would make him feel sad if he found out that you girls knew where he is. He doesn't want you to know."

Lyn looked over at Grandma and said, "I won't let Dad know that you told me about him, Grandma. I don't want to hurt his feelings." Shifting her gaze to me, she coaxed, "We won't, right, Jeri? We won't let Dad know."

Barely breathing, I nodded my head.

"Good," Grandma responded, squashing her cigarette in the ashtray. Briskly, she stood up and pressed her hands down the front of her dress to smooth out the creases. "Your mom will be here shortly," she said. "I'll tell her that we had this talk about your dad."

As far as Grandma was concerned, everything was all over, said and done.

No one asked me what it was like for me to have my dad in jail. I wasn't allowed to tell my dad how afraid I was or how sad I was that he left me.

Through the years I've tried to understand how I coped and adapted as a child being told to keep secrets about my dad and being excluded from conversations so that I was left in confusion, not knowing what was going to happen to me. I'm not blaming my grandma or my mom for not asking me how I felt. I was a kid. I know that in that time most parents, just like their parents before them, did not talk with children about "grown-up matters."

My grandmother and mother applied that rule to me, and in our case, since my father being in jail was a huge scandal, we were required to keep secrets not only from one another but from our neighbors as well. I figured that I wasn't allowed to tell anyone that my dad was in jail because that was where bad people went. My dad must be bad, I thought.

We kept our business to ourselves and went right on acting as if everything was normal. The lessons I took away from all this were that I should never speak up, that I should hide the truth no matter what, and that I should pretend I was all right even when I wasn't.

More than a decade passed before I learned why my father was in jail. In 1963 he was sentenced to serve four years in Reidsville Penitentiary in southern Georgia for leading an interstate car-theft ring with the Dixie Mafia. Only when I learned about the car-theft ring all those years later did I realize that our dad didn't buy the farm, or Mickey, for Lyn and me. Mickey was never ours, not really, and after that awful day I never saw him again. I think that what mattered most to my dad was the chop shop he was running out of that barn.

I could have felt betrayed when I found out about the car-theft ring, but I just brushed off the truth. As the years passed, I was getting better and better at stuffing down emotions that I didn't want to feel.

5

Real Good Smoker

That winter when I was ten, when Dad was in jail, and Mom and Lyn and I were living at the Peach Valley Apartments, it snowed. One morning in late November I knelt on my bed, looked out the window and slipped right back to five years earlier, reliving the morning when I was six and saw snow for the first time.

My six-year-old self woke up in my room on Alverado Way and peered out the window, mesmerized, as snowflakes drifted from the sky. A soft white layer covered everything, the trees, the swing set and the roofs of all the houses. It looked just like the winter-wonderland pictures in my fairy-tale book, as if one of those beloved stories had come to life.

Lyn and I were all set to sprint out the front door in our pajamas and fall down to roll in the snow, but Mom stopped us, her arms filled with warm clothes. When at last we were allowed out the door, I was wrapped up in two sweaters and heavy brown corduroy pants. To our utter delight, we had just taken our first tentative steps into the thick snow where the lawn should be when Daddy bolted out of the house and landed right next to us. We fell to the ground and rolled around in the snow together, laughing hysterically.

"Hey, girls," Dad said, "here's how you make a snow angel."

I jumped up and watched him sweep his arms and legs back and forth in the white powder. When he stood, I stared in wonder at the perfect winged angel shape he had left behind in the snow.

NOW, STARING OUT my window at the white blanket that covered the front lawn of our Peach Valley Apartments building, I remembered every detail of that beautiful angel, and I was gripped by sadness. Was my dad all right in jail, I wondered. Would he really come back one day to play with me and make me laugh? And if he did come back, would he be my loving fun dad or my angry dad?

A week later, when we were eating our chicken potpies on trays while we watched *Bewitched* on TV, Lyn looked over at Mom and said, "Mom, I'm a year older now and so is Jeri. We could walk home together from the bus after school and stay on our own until you get home from work. The snow is all gone. It's not slippery anymore." Before Mom could answer, Lyn went on. "We could get started on our homework sooner. Isn't that right, Jeri?"

I didn't tell Mom that, earlier in the day, Lyn had told me what she was going to say and instructed me to agree with her. I figured I wasn't really lying to our mom, just not telling her everything.

"Jeri, how do you feel about coming home to the apartment when I'm not here?"

"I think it would be okay. Lyn's old enough to take care of things until you get home. It's only two hours," I said, staring at the TV as Samantha twitched her nose and a vacuum cleaner magically appeared and flew across the room and into her waiting hands.

Mom paused. "You girls know that you have to follow the rules if you're here by yourselves. Number one is that none of your friends, especially boys, are allowed in the house. Can you promise me that you won't let your friends in the apartment?"

"Yes, Mom. We'll follow the rules," Lyn said.

Within a week of making that promise, Lyn invited our friends Cathy, Beth, Glen and Joe to come with us from the bus stop, down the expressway access road and right into the apartment. I went along with what Lyn wanted to do. It was exciting to be in the apartment without any adults. I didn't think we would get caught.

One of our favorite things to do on those unsupervised afternoons was to phone the local drugstore to ask for a free delivery. If we bought two dollars' worth of stuff, we could have cigarettes brought right to our door, no questions asked.

I already knew how to smoke. One time, months earlier, when I was spending the night at Cathy's, Dolly, a friend of Cathy's older sister, was there. After Cathy's mother left to go to her cocktail waitress job at the Sans Souci Lounge, Dolly asked me to follow her to one of the downstairs bedrooms. She opened her pack of Salem cigarettes, pulled one out and handed it to me.

"Here," she said. "I'm going to teach you how to inhale."

My hand jittered as I reached to take the cigarette. I had to do what she said. I wanted her to like me; even more, I wanted to be like her. All the older girls smoked, including my sister. Smoking, I hoped, would make me feel older and maybe even turn me from a hanger-on into one of them.

I couldn't stop staring at Dolly's bleached blonde hair, perfectly curved around her pretty face, and her long, dark red fingernails. I placed the cigarette between my lips, hoping I wasn't somehow doing even that part wrong. She flicked her metal lighter and held the flame to the end of my Salem.

In her smooth, silky southern drawl she said, "Take a little puff and then a deep breath."

I took a puff and a breath. The smoke caught in my throat and sputtered out of my mouth with each hacking cough. I peered at Dolly through watery eyes.

"Try it again," she said with a convincing, pretty smile.

I took another smaller puff and inhaled. And somehow I managed not to cough, even though my throat felt like I had swallowed the burning end of the cigarette.

"Now you're a smoker, a real good smoker," she said, nodding her head.

So when the drugstore started making those free deliveries, I knew what to do. I was a real good smoker.

THE FUN AND FREEDOM didn't last long. A month after we started hanging out with our friends in the apartment, Mom walked through the front door one afternoon and caught us. I froze, my heart racing, as her expression shifted from surprise to anger. Fortunately, our stash of cigarettes was still in a Quaker oatmeal box hidden in the top of our closet.

Mom threw her purse on the sofa, pointed to the open door and shouted, "You kids need to get out right now and don't ever come in this apartment again unless I'm here!"

I was terrified and embarrassed. After our friends scurried out the door, Mom turned on Lyn and me.

"You girls are on restriction. No friends, phone calls or spending the night out for a month!"

But two weeks later, without Mom around to enforce the rules, Lyn convinced me to ignore her. If I wanted my sister and her friends to include me, I had to be loyal to them. We let boys in the apartment and called the drugstore as if nothing had happened.

The way I saw it, Mom changed for the better after Dad was gone. Years later she told me that she felt like a burden had been lifted from her shoulders. She laughed more and did things like sing along when I played "The Girl from Ipanema" on the piano. I just hoped she would still sing songs with me if she ever found out I had disobeyed her again. I tried not to think about what getting caught would mean. My mom would disapprove of me, and that would mean that I wouldn't be her good little girl anymore.

One freezing Saturday afternoon a week after Christmas, I was sitting in the living room with the new roller skates Mom had given me, waiting for Lyn to finish putting on her makeup. We were going to Playland Roller Rink on Buford Highway about four miles from our apartment. Playland was a popular social hub where we met up with our friends to skate, hold hands with boys and watch the older kids in the Party Room dance the Twist and the Hully Gully to jukebox music.

Lyn came into the living room wearing her pair of white earmuffs. The week before, when Mom brought home a Woolworth's bag and told us to look inside, Lyn took the bag, reached in and pulled out two pairs of earmuffs. She picked the white ones and handed me the brown pair. I didn't want the brown ones either, but I knew better than to try to talk her out of what she wanted. That never worked.

"Let's go," Mom said. I put on my brown earmuffs and followed Mom out to our car, the Green Hornet.

Braking for a stoplight near the expressway overpass, Mom sang out, "I have good news, girls! I have the money. I can pay you back so you can buy that horse you were saving up for!"

I flung my arms over the front seat where she and Lyn were sitting and whooped, "Really, Mom? Can we buy a horse?"

She paused, waiting for Lyn to say something. When Lyn didn't, she finally asked her, "What do you think, Lyn? Do you want to get a horse?"

"Sure, Mom," she answered.

"Well, when the weather gets a little warmer, I'd say in a couple more months, we can go down to the stockyard and pick out your horse."

MOM KEPT HER WORD. The day I looked out my bedroom window and saw the first green buds on the dogwood tree, we got in the car and drove downtown to the stockyard.

That glorious day, Pixie came into our lives. Mom found a spot for her at a pasture not far from where we lived, so we could get there on our own after school. I loved my new role as caretaker of this gentle animal. She needed me. And looking back, I realize how much I needed her. Somehow Pixie made me feel as if our family was together again, kind of like when we all lived together on Alverado Way.

I don't know how our mother was able to scrape the money together for that horse when she was barely earning enough to cover rent and groceries, but she did it. I now know that she wanted to distract us from thinking about Dad being in jail. And for a long time she succeeded. "Also, I hoped you would spend less time thinking about boys," she told me in one of the many talks we've had over the years, revisiting the highs and lows of the Peach Valley days. "It worked for a little while, anyway."

PIXIE GAVE ME SOMETHING to write to my dad about. Just as I promised my grandma, I never let on that I knew he was in jail.

July 1964

Dear Pop! I feel fine, look fine and act fine so I guess it's true, sorry to say. I am fine. I'm going to write you about my favorite thing in the world, Pixie. The other day Lyn and I were walking down the path in the woods which leads out to the pasture. Out in the middle of the pasture was Pixie. I walked up to her and threw my arms around her. She stood still, gobbling up all the love and attention. I have been training Pixie to stand still when I get off of her and walk away. After two days, I could walk completely across the pasture and she wouldn't budge. I ran to her and petted her warmly each time she did it. Now I want to teach her to come out of the stillness and run to me when I whistle. Well, so much for this letter. I'll write another soon! Luff Ya, Ber

The letters I wrote my dad during those months didn't feel so much like lies, because every word I wrote about Pixie was true as could be.

FOUR MONTHS AFTER we got Pixie we moved to an apartment complex on the other side of the expressway: Northgate Arms. Mom told us that we needed to move because the rent had gone up at Peach Valley. We hated not having a dishwasher at the new place, and we hated toting our clothes to the laundromat, but we loved the pool that was just across the parking lot.

In June 1964, Lyn and I started summer school. Mom needed somewhere for us to be while she was at work; also, Lyn had flunked a couple of her sixth-grade classes. Still, we had more time than before to be in the pasture with Pixie.

The pasture was huge, with a forest of pines close to the road. And Pixie wasn't the only horse. We'd take turns riding the resident pony without saddle or bridle until we fell off. We'd spend hours combing Pixie, brushing her and braiding her mane and her tail. It was a quiet time. When I smelled her horse aroma my whole body tingled with a comforting kind of excitement, the kind you have when you know you're on a wild adventure. I was hooked on being outside, riding horses under a pale blue, white cloud sky. I didn't want that feeling to end.

At the start of that summer, every minute we weren't with Pixie or at school, we were at the pool. I loved swimming and riding with my sister, spending almost all my time with the person I felt closest to in the world. That was until she started being noticed by, and noticing, the boys around the place. The Northgate Arms groundskeepers were teenage boys, and when they saw Lyn in her red-striped two-piece bathing suit, they paid attention.

Gradually, Lyn shifted her own attention from me to them. I hunched by the pool in my one-piece while she did swan dives over and over again into the water, arms perfectly poised over her head, legs straight and toes pointed.

One hot Saturday morning she pranced into the living room in her two-piece.

"I'm going to the pool," she shouted as she shut the front door without asking if I wanted to come.

Dejected, I ran to the window. Sure enough, the teenage boys were at the pool, scooping out leaves with a large pole net. I couldn't watch for another second. I dashed into our bedroom, fighting back tears.

As the summer progressed, Lyn's letters to Dad were very different from mine, entirely focused on boys.

> *Dear Dad, I still have the same old boy troubles ... For a couple of weeks my boyfriend and I were having quarrels on and off. Monday he was going to break up with me and go with another girl. So today when he called he said that it was all a joke, so he said he loved me and couldn't live without me. So we made up and he said I could keep his sweater and his ring. So now I'm back on cloud 9 ... And you thought I was going to have a lot of problems with boys. WOW! I love you more than words can write so I won't even try. Your Lynie*

She turned twelve that summer, and some of her best friends were already attending Sequoyah High. She couldn't wait to hang out with them, and when school started she became less interested in being with Pixie and me. She came up with excuses why she couldn't go to the pasture after school.

"Take Cathy with you," she told me. With Dad in prison and Mom always working, Lyn was the one I clung to for some semblance of security. Maybe if I went along with her request and kept my mouth shut, she would come back to the horses and me.

One day in late October, Lyn did come with me to the horses again. I was ecstatic, but somehow we got into an argument—I don't recall what it was about—and she picked up a rock and threw it at me. As I turned to run, the rock hit me in the back of the head. I fell to the ground. Lyn rushed over to me, pulled on my arm and shouted, "We have to go, Jeri! You're bleeding!" Panicked, we walked twenty minutes to the gas station, blood trickling down my neck all the while.

I remember feeling almost out of my body with the throbbing in my head and the sensation of her pulling at me. I still have a lump from that blow. When I go to a new hair stylist or have a massage, I feel obliged to announce that the protrusion is nothing to be concerned about. "That's where my sister hit me in the head with a rock," I explain, my smile glossing over the memory of just how deeply that wound burrowed into my little-girl self. It wasn't the physical hurt that bothered me. I knew Lyn was just as shocked as I was when the rock actually hit me. It was the loss of what we had with Pixie, the shift I sensed in our relationship. Something had cracked between us, and it seemed to me that my sister didn't really want me in her life.

Years later, when Lyn and I were well into our adult lives, I wanted to understand better what it was like for her when we were teenagers. I asked Lyn how she felt about me at that time of horses and high school. She said, "You ceased to exist for me, just like pretty much everyone else. I really felt like I couldn't depend on or trust the adults in my life to take care of me.

"I was really pissed off with Mom for dating other men when Dad was in jail. I felt like she was betraying Dad, so I decided to rebel against anything she told me. I felt justified in being rebellious and taking it out on her. I realize now that I was desperate to be in control of my life no matter what the adults wanted me to do or be. I was going to do it my way. I was in my own world, trying my best to get away with whatever I wanted and what I thought I needed to be safe."

"How did boys play into your needing to take control?" I asked.

"When I figured out how to get the attention of boys, especially the older boys who had cars and money, I felt like I finally had a way out, a way to get away from the adults. What I didn't realize at first was what those boys wanted from me in return. I thought that being desired sexually meant that someone cared about me."

6

Lies

Lyn soon discovered that if she could talk our mother into letting us spend the night at Cathy's when Cathy's mom was working until two in the morning, we had hours when no adults were around. One night some of Lyn's friends, Cathy and I walked about four miles from Cathy's to a party in the Northwoods neighborhood, not far from where Grandma lived. When we got to the house and knocked, no one answered.

"They can't hear us," Lyn shouted over the blaring music. She reached over and opened the door. Cigarette smoke billowed out. The room was packed with kids dancing, making out, drinking, smoking. Beer cans, dirty dishes and garbage littered the floor and covered every surface.

We pushed our way into the room and moved toward the kitchen to see if any of our friends were there. Lyn led the way through the crowd. I tried to stay close to her, but it was tough going, and I tripped over someone's legs and tumbled to the floor. When I got back to my feet, the mass of bodies had swallowed Lyn. She was gone. And as if that wasn't enough for me to deal with, someone shouted, "Cops!"

Within seconds the panicked throng was dragging me with them out the back door. Dozens of people charged down the lawn, into a ravine and up the other side, disappearing into the dark night. My neck pulsed with the hard beat of my heart as I broke away and screamed, "Lyn! Cathy!"

Someone grabbed my hand and shouted, "Run!" I looked to find myself attached to a boy I had never seen before.

"My sister! I don't know where she is!" I screamed back at him.

"Come on! We have to get away before the cops get us!"

I tried to twist my hand out of his grip, but he pulled me with him at a gallop through the yard. We ran to the other side of the ravine and through the back streets until we were several blocks away from the party house. Gasping for breath, I stopped and bent over, holding my stomach. All around was eerily silent. I could hear nothing but our hard breathing.

Trembling, I stood straight and said, "I'm lost. I need to find my sister."

"I can walk you back to your house," he replied.

I wiped my shirt-sleeve across my wet face and took a good look at him. His straight brown hair fell over one of his eyes. He was wearing black suede ankle boots, just like I'd seen on George, my favorite Beatle.

"What's your name?" I asked.

"Jan … Jan Sandlin."

Jan walked me home that night without incident, and after that he started coming over to Cathy's every weekend to pick me up on his motorcycle and ride me all around Doraville. I was deeply flattered that a sixteen-year-old, especially one as cool as Jan, wanted to have anything to do with me. After all, I was barely twelve.

MY LETTERS TO my dad started to sound more like Lyn's.

December 19, 1965
Dear Pop,

Me and the boys are doing fine especially Jan.

We are going steady. He hasn't given me a ring yet but plans to give me a Chamblee High School ring. If I get a picture of him I'll send it to you so you can see what he looks like. Okay? Now my favorite part is about Pixie! I am a little worried about the weather. It's getting worse. Because it is winter she is getting a thick fur coat. She has gotten a bit spirited because we haven't been riding her as much, but when the weather gets better I will.

Luff ya!
Ber

January 20, 1966
Dear Daddy,

Boy! You sure better get back here cause I'm having all kinds of boy problems. Jan and I broke

> *up two weeks ago. To tell you the truth I still love him … I think I'll wait about a week and see if I can scrape up a boy and if I can't I'll just have to figure out a way to get Jan back. I have one boy in mind to try for. He's not quite as cute as Jan but a lot sweeter. I think he likes me a little bit. His name is Greg. Pixie is fine. I'm relieved because it has been so cold out. Guess I better go get ready for skating. Byeeeeeeeeeeeeeeeeeee! Jeri*

Jan and I did start seeing each other again. Now he mostly rode me on his motorcycle over the railroad tracks to the apartment in Chamblee where he lived with his mother. He also started teasing me about how he was going to be the first one to have sex with me. I had already French-kissed with other boys and, of course, was well aware of what having sex was.

As the weeks passed, the more I refused the more persistent he became.

I wasn't interested in having sex, at least not actual intercourse. We played around sexually all the time, and I liked that. I was attracted to Jan and remained intrigued and flattered by the fact that he wanted to be with me. There was something else that Jan made me feel. It was the same caring I felt as a younger girl when my dad held me lovingly in his lap, the safety and protection I felt holding his hand crossing the street. It was familiar, and with my dad away in prison, it was missing.

This playful stage went on for a good six months. I started to think that I loved Jan. I couldn't bear the thought that he would leave me.

ONE NIGHT WHEN Mom thought I was at Cathy's but I was with Jan in his room, he pinned me down on the bed and unzipped my jeans.

"What are you doing?" I blurted with a half-hearted laugh, hoping that he was just playing around.

"Come on," he pleaded, staring straight into my wide, anxious eyes. "Don't you love me?"

I had no response to that except to lie perfectly still. I heard him, loud and clear: If you love me, those beautiful intense eyes of his were saying, you'll let me do this. This is what I need from you.

I felt my underpants slide down around my ankles and before I could answer him the weight of his body landed on top of me. I tried to prepare myself, but when he pushed his hard penis inside me, it hurt, and as he pushed deeper inside me, it hurt even more. Surely this wasn't what it was supposed to be like. I tried to pull my arms up from his grip, but he was stronger than I was, and he held me down.

"Please, please. You're hurting me," I said.

In that moment I wanted him to stop, but he didn't. Instead, he put his head down and moved faster, up and down on my body, until he let out a deep moan and fell limp beside me on the bed. As I lay there with my pants down, I felt burning between my legs. The rest of my body was numb. I couldn't help fearing that now that Jan had gotten his way, he would leave. I hadn't considered that possibility until he forced himself on me against my will, until he writhed on me like I wasn't even there.

When we sat up to get dressed, he pulled me over to him, held me in his arms and pushed my hair back from my forehead just like my dad used to do.

I smiled and hugged him back. I wanted him to know that no matter how much it hurt, I would do it over and over again to please him.

And my strategy worked.

Over the next several months, Jan convinced me to ditch school so we could sneak into my family's apartment and have sex while Mom was at work. That June I graduated from elementary school. While I was on the stage getting my diploma, my teacher told my mom how glad she was to see me, since I'd been absent from so many classes recently. I had been forging notes from my mom saying I was sick. When Mom caught up with me afterward, she asked me why my teacher would say such a thing.

Terrified that the truth was about to come out, I thought fast. "I'm sure it has something to do with me switching homerooms," I told her. "The schedules were messed up for a lot of the kids."

DURING THOSE MONTHS with Jan, not much more than a year after we got Pixie, I started making excuses why I couldn't go to the pasture after school to feed my horse. And contrary to what I had written in that letter to my dad, I didn't start riding Pixie more when the weather got better. I didn't want anything, including my horse, to stop me from spending as much time with Jan as possible.

Lyn and I got into some heated discussions with Mom. We'd got to a place where we didn't seem to care about Pixie anymore. Mom threatened to sell her, but we didn't believe she would. Pixie was mad at us too. On one of the rare occasions when I tried to ride her, she took me straight into the stand of pines by the road and did her best to knock me off her back. I had no idea that my neglect was hurting her. And I was so fixated on Jan that I didn't think about what losing Pixie would mean.

The day Mom sold Pixie, all that loss filled me up and spilled over. I went to my room, threw myself down on the bed and sobbed.

AFTER I STARTED eighth grade at Sequoyah High School, I soon realized that I wasn't Jan's only girlfriend. I was stunned. My jealousy exploded into bitter arguments that usually ended with me believing Jan's lies that he wasn't with another girl. I couldn't leave him no matter how much my jealousy broke me apart and devastated my self-esteem.

That January I stopped hearing from Jan altogether, and I grew more and more terrified that he was leaving me. After a couple of weeks he called to tell me that he was in juvenile hall and wanted me to come with his mom to visit him there. The phone call was such a relief. He was in trouble, and I was the one he called. He must really love me. I had no idea that he was robbing people's houses, but I didn't care. What he'd done to end up in detention didn't matter one bit. After all, our dad went to jail, and our mom and our grandma never said a word to me about why. They just told me to keep on writing to him as if nothing had changed.

I don't remember everything about my visit with Jan, but I vividly remember waving goodbye to him as he stared out at me through a chain-link fence topped with barbed wire. As I turned away from Jan that day, I remember consciously stuffing down my sadness and fear at being separated from the person that I thought I loved.

Jan never contacted me again, and I didn't understand why. I made no attempt to visit a second time. I had no idea what happened to him until 1997, thirty years later, when my sister called me from Atlanta. "Jeri, have you seen the October issue of *People* magazine?"

With my heart in my throat, I listened as she read the article to me.

> Twenty-six years after she was blamed for her infant half-brother's death, Tracy Rhame had her name cleared when her stepfather was convicted of murder today in the case. Her stepfather, Jan Barry Sandlin, who is serving a life sentence in Florida for armed robbery, was sentenced to two life terms in prison for the 1971 beating death of 4-month-old Matthew Golder. Prosecutors say Mr. Sandlin placed Tracy, who was 2, in the baby's crib and made it look as if she had tossed the baby out. Ever since, she said she had lived with the blame and guilt, until the burden was lifted by the jury's verdict.

I remember feeling sickened that day by the pain and suffering he caused this family. I also was shocked by the realization that Jan murdered an infant only a few years after the last time I saw him. A chill ran up my spine. I could have been the girl who lost her child to his brutality.

After I hung up the phone, I couldn't help but wonder: Would I have been with someone like Jan if my dad had been around more, if he hadn't been in jail?

7

Safety Net

By the time my relationship with Jan ended, my mother and father were divorced, and she had married Bill Walker, a quiet man and a good provider who she had been seeing since not long after we moved to Northgate Arms. Dad was still away in prison, and I was desperately in need of some stability in my own life. So it turned out to be lucky for me that Lyn managed to attract Eddie, one of the guys who took care of our apartment pool, to be her steady boyfriend. I guess I should be grateful for that two-piece bathing suit after all! About a month after I made that visit to see Jan, Lyn asked if I wanted to double-date with Eddie's cousin, Steve. At eighteen, Steve was five years older than me. He had already graduated from high school while I was just in my first year.

After our first date with Lyn and Eddie, Steve asked me to go out with him again. A week later he picked me up in his silver 1966 Oldsmobile Cutlass 442. I felt really special getting into that car and riding through Doraville with Steve. I thought he was cute, with his straight blond hair and baby-blue eyes, and I hoped he thought the same about me. He took me to the church his parents made him attend every Sunday. Fifteen minutes after the service started, he winked at me and wrote on the paper program, "I can't wait for this to be over. Let's go to Shoney's and get something to eat after we get the hell out of here." That second date turned into a five-year relationship.

With Steve in my life, I felt a sense of security for the first time in three years. Mom saw that Steve was good for me, so even though he was a lot older than I was, she encouraged the relationship. She knew we were having sex, so she helped me get birth control pills.

Steve loved to sit in our living room on Friday nights and have long talks with my mother. Because he'd had a conservative southern Christian upbringing, he was intrigued by my mom's progressive, open-minded approach to life. Mom said that being from the North and having Swedish ancestry made her more of a liberal. She and Steve talked about what Mom called "the philosophy of life." She said there were important principles and values to follow in life, such as not judging others until you had walked in their shoes. She wasn't against organized religion, but she said that everyone has a right to believe what they want, and their beliefs don't make them sinners. She believed in equal and reproductive rights for women and advocated for all people, no matter their circumstances, to have opportunities to advance themselves in life.

She recommended that Steve read books by Alan Watts and Buckminster Fuller, and poems by Walt Whitman.

I sat next to Steve in that living room and soaked in every word. In retrospect, I see that my mother was mentoring me, something she continues to do to this day, at the age of eighty-eight.

I believe that if a child has just one reliable, kind person in their life, they have hope for happiness and success. A coach, teacher, pastor, friend, grandparent or parent can make all the difference for a young person who has experienced childhood trauma. I was fortunate that that person was my mother; when I was at the critical age of fourteen, my mom's encouragement was helping me build self-esteem, which made it easier for me to make healthier choices for myself. She saw my talents and abilities and ensured I saw them in myself.

"You can do anything, Jeri, as long as you work hard," she told me many times.

One hazy fall afternoon when I was just starting ninth grade at Sequoyah High, I stood alone at the top of the school steps, holding my books in my arms and waiting for Steve to pick me up. As I watched for Steve's silver car, I saw a black Pontiac Bonneville pull up and stop. A dark-haired man in a white shirt got out. When he turned and took his first steps toward the school, my heart stopped. That man was my father, no longer far away somewhere in prison, but right here walking toward me.

I watched as he briskly crossed the street and started up the steps, his loose shirt billowing around his broad chest. He looked exactly as he always had.

I didn't know what caused the knot that caught in my throat or the tears that swelled in my eyes as I waited for him to catch sight of me. I hadn't seen him in four years, and no one had told me that he was getting out of jail. I was completely unprepared. How could he show up at my school like this? I felt my worlds colliding.

As he started up the last flight of steps to the school, he caught sight of me, and his face lit with joy.

"Ber!" he called, and waved. At the sound of his voice and the sight of his loving face, happiness washed through me, mixed with my fear and confusion. With each step that brought him closer, I felt the pull of his magnetism grow stronger.

"Jeri!" He grabbed me and pulled me into his arms. My shoulders softened. "I missed you so much, Pumpkin," he said softly, pulling me closer.

"I missed you too, Dad," I said quietly. For a moment I forgot that I was on the front steps of my school, surrounded by my peers—and that Steve was going to show up at any moment—and sank into Dad's tenderness. For that moment I was a little girl again, wrapped in my father's love.

Then I remembered. My back stiffened. I stepped away and glanced down at the parking lot. There Steve was, sitting in his car waiting for me. One thing I knew for sure: I wasn't ready for Steve to meet my dad.

"Dad, I have to go now. My ride is here," I said, shifting from one leg to the other.

His face fell. "But I'm here to give you a ride," he replied, looking from me to the parking lot and back again.

"I didn't know you were coming, Dad," I said. We walked down the steps together. At the bottom I gave him one more quick hug and turned toward Steve. I felt conflicted as I walked away. When I was small, my dad was the male figure in my life who loved me and who I loved. But when he left, especially once I reached puberty and found myself turning into a teenager with my eyes on boys and friends, he grew less important to me. Because Dad had been away for years, I was more comfortable with Steve. Steve gave me what I felt my dad couldn't: someone I could rely on, someone who was there for me.

After that, Dad went right on trying to reconnect with me. He got an apartment not far from us, and he married Joyce, the woman I first met when he picked her up to go to the farm. I never got along with my stepmother. She didn't really have a chance with me. I was so close to my mom that I resented her. I visited them, but not often. It was a relationship of obligation, an awkward connection based on years of lies.

AROUND THE TIME that Dad got out of prison, Lyn and Eddie broke up. Lyn bounced back and forth between living with me at Mom's and living at Dad's apartment with him and Joyce. While I was going steady with Steve and making good grades, Lyn started dating the brother of one of her girlfriends. Randy was much older than Lyn and spent most of his time hanging out at the local pool hall.

Shortly after her sixteenth birthday, Lyn told Mom she was pregnant. Mom insisted that she and Randy get married. Lyn told me years later that she was all for getting married and moving out so she could be on her own. She dropped out of school, married Randy at the courthouse and moved into an apartment with him. She was set to have Randy's baby and live happily ever after with the boy she loved.

When Dad found out about Lyn's predicament, he said that he could arrange for her to have an abortion, which was illegal in 1968. Lyn wasn't convinced that she wanted an abortion until Randy came home from the pool hall late one night, drunk. He pulled her by her hair, punched her in the stomach, shoved her out the door and locked it, leaving her alone in the cold dark night.

Our stepmother, Joyce, drove Lyn across the state line to Alabama, where she and my dad had arranged for my sister to have an illegal abortion. Joyce then turned around and drove Lyn back to a hospital in Atlanta, where Dad paid a doctor he knew to complete the "miscarriage." My sister stayed in the hospital for a week, receiving blood transfusions. I'll never forget her pale face as she lay in the hospital bed with IV tubes hooked up to her arm. I very much wanted her to get better so she could come home with me.

When she did come home, it was just as I had hoped … for a few weeks. We shared a bed and talked and laughed into the night. She showed me how to put on makeup, how to straighten my long wavy hair by rolling it in orange-juice cans, and how to mix and match skirts with tops for my dates with Steve.

One night a month later I sat pushed up against the headboard of that bed and watched her pull clothes out of the closet and shove them into a suitcase.

"Are you crazy?" I shouted at her. I had just gotten my sister back, and now she was leaving me to return to a boy who beat her up.

"No, I'm not crazy. I love him!"

My body tensed as a rush of hot prickles shot up the back of my neck. I lunged off the bed and landed on my sister. She stumbled into the open closet. Within seconds she turned on me, grabbed my arms and dug her long hard fingernails into my forearms.

I jumped away from her and screamed, "You're crazy! Don't ever come back. I never want to see you again!"

Without another word, and with tears running down her cheeks, my sister closed her suitcase and went through the door.

I stared down at the small, red, crescent-moon-shaped marks puncturing my skin. I felt helpless. I couldn't protect my own sister, the person I loved so very much. I crawled back in the bed, pulled the covers over my head and cried.

THE CLOSER I GOT to graduation, the more obsessed I became with marrying Steve. I convinced him to buy me a diamond engagement ring, even though he didn't want to set a date or make any plans. I cut out pictures of wedding gowns, houses and babies from magazines and pasted them in my scrapbook. My entire senior year I knew that as soon as I graduated from high school I would get married and start my family.

Then the unthinkable happened.

One Saturday afternoon, Steve picked me up to go to the Varsity, a drive-in diner near Georgia Tech in downtown Atlanta. He liked going there because that was where guys would show off their hot cars. We pulled in, slowly rolled to the upper deck and parked.

We sat in the car and waited for our order, with the driver's side window partially opened. Warm spring breezes drifted in and floated around as we sat, not saying a word. Steve was unusually quiet.

"Are you okay?" I finally asked.

He only hesitated for a moment before delivering the blow. "I got drafted. I'm going to Vietnam," he solemnly said, staring out the front windshield as he spoke.

I gasped. How could my Steve be leaving me? I was stunned.

In June 1970, when I graduated from high school a year early, Steve was in boot camp at Fort Benning, Georgia. Then he was shipped off to Vietnam, where he served for a year in the U.S. Army Infantry. We wrote letters, but my life was not the same. So many days went by without Steve in them. I was only sixteen and my safety net had a big hole in it.

Steve had replaced the male attention I received from my dad as a child. Even though there were times Dad had scared me with his outbursts, I relied on the security I felt from being loved by a father, a boyfriend. Now I was like a kite floating away in the wind without anyone holding the string.

8

The Strip

A few months after Steve left, one afternoon when I was bored and lonely, I called my sister. Even though my father was around and I was living with my mother, I was way past the stage in my life when I wanted to hang out with my parents. I hadn't made many friends, and I'd lost contact with those I did have because I'd been spending all my time with Steve.

When Lyn heard my voice, she actually sounded excited. She invited me downtown to a party the next weekend.

The hippie movement that started in San Francisco's Haight-Ashbury district had finally taken hold in the conservative South. The midtown Atlanta section of Peachtree Street between Tenth and Fourteenth, called "the Strip," blossomed with flower children in their tie-dyed T-shirts, bell-bottom jeans and beads. It was all so foreign to me. I had never even smoked pot. But four days after that phone call, there I was on a Saturday night, walking along the Strip with my sister and her boyfriend. Lyn had finally gotten away from Randy and was living on Tenth Street with John, a drug dealer.

The party was at a large, lavishly decorated house that Lyn told me belonged to one of John's clients. It was filled with people dancing to loud rock-and-roll music. Lyn pulled me around the room, introducing me to one person after another. I immediately felt special and liked being there with her.

After we had been at the party for about an hour, John coaxed me into trying what he called electric punch, Kool-Aid spiked with LSD. I hesitated for a moment but reached out and took the cup. I felt I had to do what the others were doing so I wouldn't be rejected. But more than that, everyone looked like they were having the time of their lives. I wanted that too. Soon a warm, elated mood stole over me. I heard a voice from across the room. It was John.

"Jeri, look at this."

He waved his leg up and down, and as I stared at him I saw brightly colored trails waft in the air after each movement. I was mesmerized. How could this be happening?

As the night progressed, my mind and body rippled with blissful sensations. I laughed, danced and hugged everyone.

After experiencing the euphoria of LSD, I knew there was no way I was going to stay at home with my mom and stepdad. I wasn't sure exactly how I was going to live downtown like my sister, but I wasn't going to let anything stop me. I had started taking classes at DeKalb College right out of high school, and made the Dean's List my first year, but I was ready to give it all up.

When Steve returned from Vietnam, our relationship no longer worked for me. By then we'd been apart for more than a year. We were both different people now, and I was eager to move on from the known and familiar to try something new.

Lloyd was tall with thick shoulder-length black hair and blue eyes. I knew nothing about him, but that didn't matter. I liked his looks. He reminded me of Jim Morrison from the popular rock band the Doors. I was on the hunt for fun and excitement, and I wanted a cute boy to hang out with. Whenever I saw Lloyd in my math class at DeKalb College, I smiled at him. After a while I started talking to him. He was unresponsive at first, but one day he asked me if I wanted to go with him to the cafeteria to get something to eat.

A month later, Lloyd asked me to go with him to an Alice Cooper rock concert at the Atlanta Civic Center. When he picked me up, I told him that I had some ecstasy. High that night, I formed a passionate bond with Lloyd and was even more determined to get him to be my boyfriend.

What I didn't know was that Lloyd had a troubled past with drug use. My choice to offer him drugs, as innocent as that seemed to me, threw the door wide open to a life I couldn't ever have imagined.

After five sheltered years with Steve, I was out on my own in the big ol' wild world. And at seventeen, I was not yet aware of how the wrong person could take advantage of my naïvety. I was an easy target.

By the summer of 1971 I had dropped out of DeKalb College and was in my first apartment, ready to make a home with my new boyfriend. The day I helped Lloyd and his friend unpack a small U-Haul with the worn olive-green couch Mom gave me from her downstairs den, my bed, a card table to use as a dining table and some plastic lawn chairs, I was elated. I was oblivious to the dirty noisy streets and looming danger of downtown.

I was finally free. Or so I thought.

A week after we moved in together, Lloyd went out by himself. I busied myself by flipping through recipes in the Betty Crocker cookbook I had borrowed from my mom. Around nine o'clock, I got stoned and put on Lloyd's leather bomber jacket. I pulled it around my body, imagining that he was holding me in his arms, and strolled out in the dark night under the canopy of the cypress trees that lined our street. The excitement of having my own place with Lloyd lifted my feet into a skip and an occasional twirl, but I was still careful not to trip on the uneven sidewalk pushed up by huge tree roots.

I waited up for Lloyd for a long time, but when he hadn't come back by midnight, I decided to go to bed. I couldn't sleep. Those jubilant moments twirling under the cypress trees warped into a painful knot in my stomach that pulled tighter and tighter hour after hour until the sun poured into the bedroom through the dusty, broken blinds. I knew he was cheating on me. I was so angry. We had just gotten our place and he was out with someone else. I jumped up and flipped over the card table. After I threw what dishes, pots and pans we had into a shambles in the living room, I fell to the floor and cried, holding my head in my shaking hands.

This wasn't the first time I'd had an uncontrollable bout of jealousy. Once when I thought Steve had cheated on me, I took a bottle of green pills. When I told Steve what I had done, he rushed me to the ER. We sat in the hospital parking lot, waiting to see if anything was going to happen to me. When nothing did, we went home. I vomited for a couple of days and had diarrhea for a week. But something in me felt satisfied. I had got his attention. Maybe he wouldn't risk me taking pills again, and that would keep him faithful.

I wasn't sure how I could make Lloyd be faithful to me, but after an hour I put everything back in its place. I was more afraid that he would leave me if he knew how crazy jealous I was. When Lloyd showed up later that day, I tried to control my shaking body as I asked him where he was all night. He confessed that he had been with his ex-girlfriend, but assured me that they didn't have sex. I wanted to believe him. I had worked so hard to make my dream come true, and I wasn't about to go back and live with my mother. I would just have to try even harder to make him love me and me only. I didn't figure out until much later that he simply got better at hiding his rendezvous with other girls.

Lloyd and I had a newspaper route for a while; then I got a job working in a gas station. That fall I enrolled in Georgia State University, a few blocks from where we lived. I was taking only one class, literature. I studied William Blake poems during the day and got stoned with Lloyd at night.

I used college to conceal, especially from Mom, how my life was changing due to the influences of the Strip.

Lloyd turned me on to the music of Bob Dylan and Richie Havens, whose songs protested the Vietnam War. I watched women burning their bras during equal rights demonstrations in Piedmont Park, and I marched in grassroots campaigns against the war. I chose to believe that drug use was one of the ways the counterculture rebelled against the establishment, and I didn't see anything wrong with it. I couldn't understand why drugs were illegal. I didn't think they were hurting anybody.

WITHIN A FEW short months, Lloyd was shooting up cocaine. He was fascinated with using needles to get high. I never did it to myself, but I let Lloyd shoot me up. Needles were more of a fringe activity, and Lloyd was moving into that fringe, with me right there alongside him. At first it seemed fun, but as the days went by, Lloyd spent all our money and all his time looking for and using drugs. I didn't realize that he was also using heroin.

I suspect that my sister told Dad she was concerned about me. One day he showed up at my apartment out of the blue. Before I answered the door, I ran into the bedroom and put on a long-sleeved shirt to cover up the bruises on my arms.

When I opened the door, he walked right in and hugged me.

"Jeri, I rented an apartment downtown," he said, pushing my hair back from my forehead. "I'd like for you to come over so we can spend some time together."

By this time, Grandpa Bert and Dad were partners in a business venture, with offices in the Atlanta Peachtree Center Towers, not far from where I was living.

"I'm okay, Dad. Don't worry about me," I replied.

"Just know I'm close by. Here's a key and the address."

Looking back, of course I wasn't okay, but I also wasn't confident and self-aware enough to tell my father the truth or even to know that I could say no to Lloyd and IV drugs. I didn't realize how often I said, "I'm okay," when it wasn't true. I continued to use the survival behaviors I had learned as a child to cover up my uncomfortable emotions in an attempt to control what was happening around me.

A week later, Lloyd asked me to take him to Dad's apartment when we knew Dad wasn't there. Even though I told him no, he had little trouble persuading me.

"I just want to see your dad's place. Ya know, how he lives. No big deal," he said with a smile.

When we got there, he looked around the living room and then went into Dad's bedroom.

"Lloyd, what are you doing?" I asked, alarmed.

"I'm just checking out the place."

I followed and watched him kneel next to the bed, pull out a briefcase and open it.

"Hey, look at this. These are phony credit cards," Lloyd said, holding up several cards. I peered at them and my chest tightened. None of the cards had my dad's name on them. I watched Lloyd put a couple of the cards in his shirt pocket.

"You can't do that!" I snapped.

"Why not? Your dad most likely stole them."

In that moment I realized my father was still breaking the law, still being a criminal, even after he spent time in jail that I thought had changed him. My legs went weak, and I felt like the room was moving in around me, closer and closer, until I could hardly take a breath.

I was relieved when Lloyd grabbed my hand and in a low voice said, “Let’s get out of here.”

PART II

1972–1999

9

Santa Cruz

In August 1972, shortly before I turned nineteen, Lloyd told me that a dealer friend of his wanted us to come to Boulder, Colorado, to party with him. I told Mom that I was going with Lloyd to enroll at the University of Colorado, Boulder, which I actually intended to do. What I didn't know until Lloyd told me when we were miles away from Atlanta was that he needed to get out of town because some guys he had ripped off were looking for him.

I hadn't spent much time with my dad over the four years since his release from prison, and I was surprised at his reaction when I phoned to tell him I was moving to Colorado.

"Ber, please don't go," he said, his voice cracking. "Your family is here, and we want you here with us."

"Dad, don't worry about me. I'm sure I won't be gone long," I said, hoping to stop him before he said anything that might stir up doubts about my decision.

Days later, when I hugged my mom goodbye, my cheerful facade crumbled. She held me in her arms for a long time. She didn't try to convince me to stay. That was not her way. She just asked me to question myself and do what I felt was right for me.

While I wasn't so sure what was right for me, I knew that I had to pretend to be happy with Lloyd's choices if I didn't want him to leave me. Doubts or no doubts, off we went, with Lloyd behind the wheel and me in the passenger seat. We drove for two days straight, compliments of Dad's stolen gas credit cards and the Pontiac Tempest convertible that my grandmother had given me.

We did party with the dealer in Boulder, which amounted to shooting up as much MDA, a type of ecstasy, as we could for a couple of days. Soon, though, we ditched the plan to stay in Boulder and headed to Aspen, where we lived for a month, selling drugs. There we had an authentic Colorado experience, sitting in the front row at a John Denver concert while he sang "Rocky Mountain High," which we definitely were.

I had never seen mountains, especially ones as magnificent as the Rockies. Many mornings I hiked by myself on hillside trails, listening to the aspen leaves quivering in the wind. When the first snows covered the town with white powder, the locals told us we'd better leave or the snow would trap us there for the whole winter. Our money was running low, so we decided we had to move on. Reluctantly, I packed up my suitcases and the feathers and stones I had collected, and we drove twelve hundred miles to Eugene,

Oregon, where we planned to find jobs and establish residency before applying to attend the state university.

We had just enough money to pay the first month's rent for an apartment near downtown. Lloyd looked for work but mostly found drugs to use and sell. I landed a job as a cocktail waitress at Step-Down-A-Go-Go, a topless bar.

A month into the plan, Lloyd got restless. With the money I had earned, we took off again. Lloyd wanted to head to Los Angeles, California. We drove for almost nine hours before we pulled over to look at the map and discovered we had just passed San Francisco. Lloyd said he wanted to go to a beach town he had been to before, which was less than two hours farther south.

On a warm afternoon in November 1972, we got to the quaint, village-like downtown area of Santa Cruz, California. Lloyd parked the car and we walked into the Catalyst, a laid-back, rustic restaurant bar. The young men had long hair and the girls wore macramé tops and floor-length skirts made of soft cotton in shades of purple and blue. Within an hour I knew I wanted to stay in Santa Cruz, though I couldn't explain why. I got up and approached the bartender.

"What do people do to make a living here?" I asked.

"You're either an artist or you sell drugs."

I thought, Well, we sell drugs. That means we'll make it here.

"Let's get a room for the night and get back on the road in the morning," Lloyd said when I sat back down.

My mind raced. I didn't want to get back on the road. In some quirky intuitive way, I knew I was exactly where

I was supposed to be. But how was I going to speak up for myself, for what I needed? Until that moment I had followed wherever Lloyd took me, even down the dangerous road of injecting drugs. I had done whatever it took to keep him from leaving me.

I took the last bite of my macaroni salad in silence. Lloyd got up and slipped on his black leather jacket.

"Come on. Let's get out of here."

I didn't budge.

"Let's go, Jeri," he said, this time a bit louder.

I sat up straight, glared at him and with the strongest voice I could muster replied, "Lloyd, I really like this place. Let's check it out for a while. We can find a room in a house or an apartment with the money I have and then look for jobs."

He stared at me for a long moment.

"Really? You want to stay in Santa Cruz? I think we'll have a better chance finding jobs in a bigger city."

I didn't give up. "I know. But I think we should try. We can always leave if it doesn't work out."

Lloyd sat back down.

Almost fifty years later I'm still living in my beloved Santa Cruz. I believe that my intuition and my willingness to speak up for myself that long-ago day saved my life.

WE RENTED A SMALL, upstairs room in a house with five other people, close to the yacht harbor. I could see the sailboats from the window. I put up sheer orange curtains and got a desk so I could write letters to my mom. Mom told me that she would send me one hundred dollars a month if I enrolled in school. I signed up for the spring semester at Cabrillo Junior College and started classes.

Soon after I formed friendships with the people who lived in the house, Lloyd decided we should get our own apartment. His drug habit was getting worse and worse, and he needed more privacy. At the same time, I was backing off from wanting to use drugs to get high.

After we moved, I was isolated once again. He would take me with him down to the Beach Flats to cop drugs. Then we'd come back to the apartment and he would shoot up. I was miserable. We fought more and more. One night after getting drunk at the Catalyst, we got into a vicious fight and screamed at one another the whole way home. When we got inside the apartment, Lloyd hit me in the face, grabbed me and threw me to the floor. I crawled to the bed and passed out.

When I woke up the next day and saw the horrifying image of myself in the mirror, with a black eye and swollen lip encrusted with dried blood, I knew I had to leave Lloyd. But how?

The only strategy I knew was to find another boyfriend who would rescue me.

I had met Tom when Lloyd and I were still living in the harbor household. He came to visit a friend, one of the other renters, and I felt an attraction to him right away. He had wavy brown shoulder-length hair, soft full lips and bright sparkling eyes. Tom was an artist with a studio in the Santa

Cruz Mountains, where he drew, painted and made redwood burl tables.

"I'm a mountain man," he told me proudly when we talked. He showed up every now and then in a soiled flannel shirt, driving an old, dented, baby-blue Chevrolet pickup truck with his German shepherd named Bush in the back. He always smiled when he saw me. Being a mountain man meant something to Tom: a couple of years earlier he had fled from the materialism of Los Angeles, where he was raised. He cared about nature and art. I had never met anyone like him.

THAT MORNING, WITH my swollen lip and black eye, I got in the car and drove to Tom's studio in the town of Boulder Creek. When I told him what had happened, he pulled me to him.

"You can stay with me if you want," he whispered in my ear and kissed me on my flushed cheek.

I went back to my apartment, got my things and opened a new chapter in my life in the arms of a caring, kind man with the Pacific Ocean on one side and the redwood forests on the other. I had not yet learned to stand on my own two feet, but at least Tom was a much better partner for me than Lloyd.

Within a couple of months, Lloyd went back to Atlanta. I have often reflected that the only good thing Lloyd ever did for me was get me to Santa Cruz, but that was a pretty good thing!

Me and Tom in Santa Cruz in 1973.

WITH LLOYD OUT OF the picture, I soaked up the progressive vibes of artists, activists and nature lovers in this lively seaside town.

I dropped my academic courses at the junior college and began taking modern dance classes instead. Dancing opened me to the exhilaration of creative self-expression. When I wasn't swaying to the rhythm of the waves and wind at the beach, I was in the studio rehearsing for a Cabrillo summer musical. I got a part-time job at Polar Bear Ice Cream Parlor near Capitola Beach, and I made redwood planter boxes with Tom in his studio long into the nights. I rode my rusty bike everywhere, sometimes stopping to read *Be Here Now* by Ram Dass in a forest meadow, lying under the blue sky on my trusty green wool army blanket.

I was in my early twenties and far away from my childhood and teenage days back in Georgia. As time went on I started feeling less afraid and more secure within myself. I still had a long way to go, but my creative artist friends and the peaceful beauty of nature were helping me to discover who I was and what made me happy. A year into our relationship, when Tom told me that he wanted to break it off, I felt strong enough to be on my own without racing out to find a new boyfriend.

10

A Plan on a Napkin

Dad continued to call me from time to time. During one of those conversations, I was surprised when he told me that he had started a new business exporting construction equipment to South America. I asked him about his business with Grandpa, and he said that they were no longer working together. He also told me he was planning to move to Cali, Colombia, and as soon as he got settled, Lyn and Joyce were moving there to live with him. He said that he would like me to think about moving there too, which I had no interest in doing.

In April 1974, a letter arrived *Express Entrega Inmediata* (Special Delivery) in my mailbox. It was from the United Corporation, Avenida 2-73, Cali, Colombia. I recognized my father's handwriting.

As I felt the thin paper of the airmail envelope in my hand, a dull throb started in my stomach.

With reluctance, I opened the letter.

> *To my baby girl,*
>
> *Well I was hoping to be back in the States by now but everything is very slow here. The house is about finished. We moved in over the weekend. I want to see you soon. Miss you not being around. Hope you will want to come here. The city is modern. The house is big, Spanish style. 7 Bedrooms, 5 baths, servants' quarters, 2 kitchens, swimming pool, gardens, patios. You'll like it.*
>
> *Miss my baby. Come and be with your Daddy. Lyn is here. She wants you to come too! Will call you next week and wire you the money to make the trip.*
>
> *Love you much. (Learn Spanish)*
>
> *Your Daddy*

As I put the letter back in the envelope, my mind knotted with confusion. I was content sharing a house with four other people on Garden Street in Santa Cruz, riding my bike to modern dance classes. Yet this letter stirred up something inside me. I wasn't drawn by his description of the luxurious house with a swimming pool. It was his words of affection that reached me: "Miss my baby. Come and be with your Daddy." Despite leaving my family to put down new roots in California, despite feeling so at home in Santa Cruz and, in some ways, feeling happier than I had ever been, reading that my father wanted to see his younger daughter awoke a longing in me that ached for his attention.

Classes at the junior college would be ending soon for summer break. I was ready to quit my job at Polar Bear Ice Cream Parlor. The timing was just right for me to leave for a month or even two or three. I was curious about what it would be like to reconnect with my family in a new and exotic place. Maybe it would be better than when I was in Atlanta. Maybe it would be better with my dad.

The next morning I dressed, pulled my long auburn hair back with a tie-dyed scarf, picked up the letter from my bedside table and walked into the kitchen where one of my roommates was cutting up carrots to juice for breakfast.

"Eddie," I said emphatically, "I'm going to South America."

Three short weeks later I was on a plane, traveling to meet my dad in Florida. After a five-hour, nonstop flight across the country, I landed at the Miami International Airport right on schedule.

I descended the metal staircase from the plane, walked across the tarmac and entered the lobby. My heart flip-flopped as I surveyed the crowd and didn't see my dad. Had something prevented him from meeting me? It wouldn't be the first time.

I looked around for a payphone, stepped past some people who were talking to the ticket agent and stopped, overcome with relief and joy. There was Dad, striding toward me in beige slacks and a light-blue short-sleeved Lacoste polo shirt. His arms were muscular and tanned. Yep. There he was, my handsome dad, looking like a movie star.

In that moment I was proud it was me he was there to meet. I hadn't thought much about Dad since I had been in

California, but as soon as my eyes landed on him, they filled with tears. And when he saw me, his preoccupied expression was replaced by a brilliant white smile. His arm flew up to wave.

"Ber!" he shouted. Seconds later he was hugging me. "Are you okay? How was the flight?"

"The flight was great. No problems," I replied.

"Well, I sure am glad you came. Lyn is really excited. You'll like it down there," he said.

As we turned to walk toward the baggage claim, he reached out to hold my hand. With the warm, reassuring grip of his hand around mine, my doubts vanished. When I was by his side and within his reach, I allowed myself to believe that everything was going to be okay. I was with my daddy!

He put my suitcase in the trunk of the car, and we drove past white sand beaches and palm trees swaying in the soft afternoon breeze. At last he turned the car into the entrance of the Fontainebleau Miami Beach and stopped in front of the valet. I gazed out at the white marble stairs leading up to massive gold doors being opened and closed by handsome doormen in black suits.

"Wow!" I exclaimed. "This place is fancy." I slumped down in the seat, not wanting to emerge from the car in my worn-out Birkenstock sandals and baggy jeans.

"Only the best for my baby," Dad said, reaching into the back seat for his briefcase.

The bellman put my small fuchsia-and-mustard-paisley suitcase on a cart and pushed it through the lobby and into the elevator, with Dad and me following. When we reached the twelfth floor, he wheeled the cart down the hall and opened a door. Blinking several times, I walked into the poshest hotel suite I had ever seen or imagined. Gold velvet curtains were pulled open, revealing expansive views of the aqua-blue Atlantic Ocean. Huge bouquets of white roses adorned the coffee table and a bureau under an ornate gold-framed mirror. Champagne waited for us on ice.

The bellman smiled at me and placed my suitcase on the floor. "Is there anything else I can do for you, Mr. Rosenthal?" he asked my dad.

"We are all set here," Dad replied, handing him a twenty-dollar bill.

The man took the money, pushed the cart out and closed the door.

Dad looked at me with that confident smile of his. "What do you think, Ber? Does this meet with your approval?"

I peered past my overgrown bangs, cleared my throat and stuttered, "This place is amazing, amazing."

I didn't want Dad to see how uneasy I felt, so I turned away from him, walked across the gleaming marble and stared out at the ocean. Since arriving in California, I had lived a simple life. My artist friends and I shunned materialism. I slept on a mattress on the floor and bought my clothes from a second-hand store.

I stepped through the door to the balcony and gulped in a huge breath of salty sea air.

"Jeri, you must be hungry," Dad called.

I turned and walked back inside.

"They have a pretty good restaurant here in the hotel. They serve Cuban food. Have you ever had a fried plantain?"

During dinner, Dad started in on his pitch to convince me to move to Colombia.

"I think you should be closer to your family, Ber. Lyn really misses you. You don't have anything going on in California, do you? You're just taking dance lessons?"

I writhed in my chair, saying nothing. I didn't tell him how much dance meant to me; I didn't say that dance was my passion, my life. I just stared at the plantain that I didn't want to eat and listened to Dad go on and on without once looking up to meet his eyes.

AFTER HE SIGNED the bill, he gave me the key to the suite and told me to go up by myself.

"I have a couple of calls to make," he explained.

When I got back to the room, I crawled into the king-sized bed, pulled the gold satin bedspread over my head and closed my eyes.

The next thing I remember was hearing Dad's voice calling me. "Jeri, where are you?"

Startled, I jerked up and revealed myself. "I'm here, Dad," I blurted out. "I must have fallen asleep."

"Oh, I didn't see you there," he said, crossing the room and sitting on the edge of the bed. "Ber, give me your passport so I can buy your plane ticket. We can get you on a flight in the morning."

"Passport?" I asked.

"Yes. I need your passport to buy your ticket, since you'll be traveling out of the country."

A sense of dread swept over me. I looked down at the crumpled bedspread and said, "I don't have a passport." My mind swarmed with anxious thoughts. Should I have known that I needed a passport? Why didn't Dad tell me? He knew that I had never been out of the country before.

"You don't have a passport?" He sounded stunned.

"I didn't know I was supposed to have a passport," I said.

"Well, of course you need a passport, Ber. I thought you knew that." His voice dropped off as he stood up, turned and walked away.

"What are we going to do, Dad?" I asked.

"I'll figure something out," he said, reaching for the phone on the nightstand. "Get some sleep. We'll work on it tomorrow, Ber."

I slumped back under the covers.

The next day after breakfast I rode around with my father while he drove us through the industrial port district of Miami. He was working. We went over railroad tracks and past rusting warehouses.

Dad parked the car under a freeway overpass and said, "Wait here. I'll be out in a few minutes." He pushed the car door shut and went inside a small office building with bars on the windows.

I took a long, tired breath and looked through the dusty windshield at the door where Dad had disappeared. I was pretty sure he was doing something illegal. I suspected it had something to do with drugs. It wasn't hard for me to put two and two together. Colombia was the cocaine capital of the world. Miami was where most of the drugs came into the United States. And I was in Miami with my father, who was trying to fly me to his home in Colombia.

Sweat rolled down the back of my neck. I leaned my head against the car window and closed my eyes. Maybe when I open them I won't be in Miami with my father anymore, I thought. At least with my eyes closed I could pretend.

That night, Dad told me that he was going to have to leave me at the hotel while he had a dinner meeting. "Just call room service," he said over his shoulder from the door.

The door clicked shut and I was alone. I plopped down on the bed and sat with my back against the wall, staring at nothing. I had come all this way to be with my dad, but now I was in the room by myself, and I had become a big problem for him because he couldn't get me on a plane out of Miami.

A surge of boiling heat rushed through me. My gaze settled on Dad's impeccably polished Bally shoes, neatly lined up in the closet. Swept up in a typhoon of frustration, I leapt off the bed and ran across the room.

"You're just a sleazy criminal!" I yelled to no one but myself. "Why, Dad? Why does it have to be this way? You care more about your fucking business than you do me!" Hot tears streamed down my face as I flung one shoe after another through the air.

When there were no more shoes to throw, I crumpled into a ball on the marble floor, grabbed my knees to my chest and rocked back and forth. When at last I sat up, I was stunned at the mess I'd made. Dad could come walking through the door any minute. I stood.

Swiping the back of my hand across my face, I crossed the room, picked up the shoes one by one and arranged them back in the closet. I washed my face, brushed my teeth and turned on the TV as if nothing had happened. Twenty minutes later I heard Dad's key in the door.

"Did you get something to eat?" he asked.

"No," I said in a flat voice. "I'm going to sleep now."

"Are you okay, Ber?" he asked.

"Sure, Dad. I'm fine. I'm just tired."

I didn't ask him if he was smuggling drugs. I didn't tell him how much I wanted his attention. I didn't ask him if he thought I was a burden because I was stupid for not bringing my passport. I just rolled over and went to sleep.

What I didn't know then but see clearly now: I was not only lying to my dad but also being dishonest with myself. I didn't want to experience my feelings of confusion, disappointment and sadness. It just seemed easier and more obvious to blame my dad for making me feel so horrible. I thought that if he were different, better than he was, certainly not a criminal, I would be better too.

I was angry that I wasn't getting what I wanted, but I thought being angry was wrong. It sure felt that way when I saw my dad get angry. I never shared with him how I felt. I never asked for what I needed. I didn't know how. I just expected him to know my needs, and when he didn't, I resented him.

On our third day in Miami, with no passport in sight, Dad revised his strategy. Over breakfast he took out a pen and drew a diagram on the back of a napkin.

"Jeri," he said, "we need to get you to Colombia, and here is how we can do it without a passport. I got you a ticket. When your plane lands at the Cali airport, the passengers will deplane and walk this way." He drew a blue line on the napkin. "When you get off, you will go this way instead. Don't worry. There will be people milling around. It won't look obvious." He spoke calmly as if what he was telling me to do was the easiest thing in the world.

"Won't you be there?" I asked.

"No," he replied. "I have more to do here, but I'll be there soon."

He drew a blue square on the napkin. "Walk over to this side of the building," he said, marking one side of the square, "go up the stairs, open the door and you'll be inside the airport. Here are a couple of phone numbers, just in case."

He wrote two numbers on the napkin.

"Just in case what?" I asked.

"Nothing's going to happen, Ber. Everyone knows me there. These numbers are for people I know at DAS, the Colombian police. They will help you," he assured me.

He handed me the ticket and the diagram of his plan to smuggle me into Colombia. I looked at him with his easy smile and relaxed demeanor. It didn't occur to me to resist him..

"Okay," I said. My heart was racing. With trepidation I folded up the napkin, put it in my purse and walked out of the restaurant. Within hours I was settling into my window seat for the four-hour trip to Cali, my paisley bag tucked into the overhead compartment.

After takeoff I distracted myself by making small talk with the man sitting next to me.

"I'm going to visit my family in Colombia. I've never been outside the United States before. Do you live there?" I asked, not even hearing his response.

I retrieved my book from my carry-on bag and read the same sentence over and over again. Removing the napkin from my purse, I studied it, trying to reassure myself that avoiding customs in Colombia would be as easy as Dad had made it out to be. All I had to do was follow the line on the napkin that curved away from where everyone else would be walking. There would be people milling around. I wouldn't be noticed.

I watched the sky flame red tinged by shades of purple and then darken to black for the last hour of the trip. I stared out into the pitch-darkness until I made out the faint glow of city lights in the distance.

The blaring static of the intercom made me jump, and the Spanish words that followed meant nothing to me. The plane swayed as it got closer to the ground, and strips of landing lights cascaded down the tarmac. Within a few moments the wheels touched down and I was in South America. Illegally.

The plane came to a stop, the doors opened and the passengers stood up, gathered their belongings and slowly made their way down the aisle. When it was my turn to exit, I took a quick survey of the tarmac from my vantage point at the top of the stairs. The passengers who had disembarked before me were walking in a line toward customs. The passengers behind me were waiting for me to move along. There was no one milling around down there. What was I supposed to do? With my heart pounding in my chest, I gripped my paisley bag.

The momentum of the people behind me got me moving again. I descended the stairs, stepped onto the tarmac and walked along with the rest of the passengers until I was about two hundred feet from the building.

Somewhere in my frozen brain I heard "Now!" I held my breath and curved away from the line.

At any moment I expected to hear someone shouting for me to stop. I walked faster. No one shouted. No one followed. Like a character in a James Bond movie, I slid into the shadows of the building that until now had been a blue square on a napkin. Fueled by adrenaline, I broke into a run, following the wall of the building and looking for the staircase Dad had told me about. I saw the bright lights of the lobby above me. There. The staircase.

Panting with fear, I lifted my bag clear of the steps, scrambled to the top and reached for the door. It was locked.

Adrenaline turned to liquid terror. I scurried back down the stairs and sprinted on along the wall, grateful for the shadows of the building. Still no one shouted at me to stop and turn myself in. I rounded the corner. Just ahead I saw another staircase. That had to be the one. Up I went, reached for the door handle, palm sweating, and pulled with all my strength. It too was locked.

The only thing separating me from the airport lobby was a thick pane of glass. Just as I was about to turn and run back down the stairs, a man in the lobby saw me and started toward the door. Through the glass I faked a relaxed smile. To my utter disbelief, he pushed the door open and nodded his head for me to come in. I entered the lobby from the runway as if it happened all the time. Maybe it did, just like Dad said.

"Thank you, thank you, gracias!" I said, laughing perhaps a little too loudly.

In my Birkenstocks and with my brightly patterned bag I stood out in the Cali airport, but I tried to act nonchalant as I searched for a payphone to call Lyn. Two men in uniform passed me. One of them stopped, turned, pointed to my suitcase and said something in Spanish. I couldn't understand him, but the expression on his face made me think he suspected something. Was I going to need one of those phone numbers Dad had scribbled on the napkin I had tucked in my purse?

The man looked at me sternly and then at his companion, saying something else in Spanish. I smiled at them, doing my best to exude confidence.

I was trying so hard to appear innocent and stupid that I almost collapsed with relief when I looked up and saw my sister and my stepmother descending a flight of stairs from a second-story waiting area. They hadn't seen me.

"Lyn!" I shouted, waving my arm.

She looked at me in disbelief, smiled and came running down to greet me. The two officers shrugged, turned and walked away.

My sister grabbed me into a hug. "We were waiting for you," she said. "We saw your plane land. Everyone went through customs and you weren't there. We were just about to leave. Where were you?"

As we drove to the house on the outskirts of town, my tight shoulders relaxed. I could finally breathe in the balmy air, knowing that I was safe in a car far away from the airport. I stared out the window, transfixed by the chaos: people walking, some with baskets or boxes on their shoulders; carts pulled by donkeys and horses mixed in with bicycles, mopeds, ancient buses and speeding cars. It was unlike any place I had ever been.

At the house, Elsa, the housekeeper, showed me to my room. She placed my suitcase in the closet and said something that I didn't understand. I shrugged. I hoped I would get used to the awkward feeling of being unable to talk to people or understand what they said to me. She smiled and disappeared onto the walkway that ran around the courtyard.

I was now standing in one of the seven bedrooms Dad had described in his letter. Finally alone, I lay down on the bed and drifted off to sleep.

I awoke to Lyn's voice. "Hey, Jeri."

I sat up and rubbed my eyes. Lyn was standing by the door.

"I'm really glad you're here," she said. "You'll meet my boyfriend, Richard, tonight. Remember I wrote you that I had an American boyfriend who was in the Peace Corps.

He's coming to pick us up around nine. We're taking you out to the best salsa dance club in Cali, the Hunca Munca. I figured you'd love to go dancing."

"Okay," I said, but then remembered that I hadn't packed a nightclub outfit. I really didn't own any.

Lyn knew me well. "You can wear something of mine," she said. "Get up. There's food for us in the kitchen."

By NINE THIRTY I was sipping a shot of aguardiente, the Colombian version of tequila, to the loud, pulsating rhythms of salsa music. It was all hips and high heels on the dance floor; I was mesmerized. Lyn grabbed my hand and pulled me up to dance with her. She looked so sexy with her long blonde hair, tight white pants and gold platform sandals.

A handsome boy nodded at me. I glanced over at Lyn and read her lips: "Dance with him!" My feet moved to the upbeat salsa rhythm as he got closer to me. I danced with him until two in the morning. Diego became my Colombian boyfriend. Even though he only spoke Spanish and I only English, we were inseparable for the two months I lived in Cali.

One night I was sitting on the couch with Diego, watching TV without understanding a word, when Lyn and Richard rushed into the room. Dad was at the dining table with Joyce.

"Dad!" Lyn shouted. "We just saw some men breaking into your office. They were taking the furniture out and putting it in a truck."

Dad, me, Joyce, Lyn and Richard having dinner together in Cali, Columbia.

Dad jumped up, ran into his bedroom and came racing out with a pistol strapped to his waist. Diego and I got up to follow him, but Joyce told us to stay put.

An hour later, Dad returned.

"What happened, Dad?" Lyn asked.

"I caught the guys and made them put the stuff back. It was Larry. That bastard."

"Who's Larry?" I asked.

"One of my business partners."

I wondered briefly why a person's business partner would try to steal his furniture. It didn't make sense to me, maybe because there was a lot I didn't know.

When, shortly after that incident, Dad told Lyn, Joyce and me that we needed to go back to the States, I suspected that this might be because he could handle things better without us around. Later I understood that it probably wasn't safe for us to be there. Dad was in the early days of what soon escalated into a very dangerous business.

Somehow Dad managed to get me a temporary passport, and two weeks after the break-in, Joyce, Lyn and I were on a plane to Miami without him. I returned to Santa Cruz, and my sister and our stepmother moved to Las Vegas to be near family friends.

11

Sisters

In the summer of 1976, a year after our return from South America, I received a phone call from my sister that changed the course of our lives.

After living in Las Vegas for a year, Joyce had decided to relocate to Florida. Lyn didn't want to move to Florida or back to Atlanta, where our mom was still living.

"Go be with your sister," Dad told her on the phone when he called her from South America. "I want my two-both to be close to each other. You're meant to be together."

While my trip to Colombia didn't change my relationship with my dad as I had hoped, I did reconnect with my sister, and that felt really good. Hence, Lyn's call to me. She explained her situation and wanted to know if she could come live with me in Santa Cruz. I didn't have to think about it. Of course she could!

While Lyn was used to a rather posh, glamorous lifestyle in Las Vegas, I was a humble hippie. I lived with my best friend, Ellen, in a small one-bedroom apartment in Capitola, a quaint, colorful village three blocks from the beach. I was excited that Lyn was coming but a bit worried about how it was going to work out.

Lyn showed up from the San Francisco airport in a limo.

"Welcome to our beachside abode!" I said, excited and nervous as I reached out to hug her. I introduced her to Ellen, and the three of us toted her bags into the living room. She put her Gucci handbag on the kitchen table and looked around the room. Macramé wall hangings and a poster of the Grateful Dead adorned the walls, which were painted light violet. A twin mattress with a brightly colored batik spread served as our couch.

"You really are a hippie, aren't you?" she said, smiling.

"I told you, big sister, but don't worry. You'll be comfortable here." I walked into the bedroom, opened my knitting basket and retrieved my baggie of primo California-grown sinsemilla weed. Within minutes we were passing the pipe and reminiscing about our two months together in South America. My time in California and hers in Colombia had given us more appreciation for one another, even with our differences. I was thrilled that she had decided to live with me. It was a homecoming of sorts.

I saw myself as my sister's adviser, helping her figure out how to survive in my fine, funky town. "You have to apply for food stamps," I told her. "I'll take you to the food stamp office.

Fill out the application. Put down that you are unemployed and you don't have any bank accounts, cash on hand or help from any relatives. Then you can get vouchers for free food. It's easy."

She made a face, like she was doubtful it would be so easy. "Are you sure?" she asked.

"Yes," I replied. "My friends and I are all on food stamps. We've never had any problems."

That afternoon, while Lyn applied for food stamps, I sat in the car and added some more rows of Jamaican Rasta colors, gold, green and red, to the beanie cap I was knitting.

An hour later she opened the car door and said, "Mission accomplished, Ber. I filled out an application for a job at the Cooper House downtown. They told me that in order to get food stamps I have to look for a job."

"I know. You just kind of fake the looking-for-a-job requirement. If you go for an interview, you just make it so they wouldn't hire you. Act spaced out and uninterested in the job."

"Oh," she said. "Okay."

Two days later I drove her downtown for the interview. The Cooper House, a historic 1890s courthouse remodeled into a retail center in the 1960s by Max Walden, was a popular landmark for locals and tourists. When I dropped her off, the sounds of Warmth, a jazz band that frequently jammed at the outdoor café, spilled into the street and through my open car window. I parked and went back to dance with some of Santa Cruz's colorful characters on the sidewalk, a typical downtown spectacle.

Lyn was gone longer than I would have thought necessary to be told she wasn't qualified for the job. Eventually she strolled out through the café.

"I got the job," she said.

"What?" I blurted. "What did you do that for?"

"I wanted it," she said. "You know me, Ber. I like nice things and that takes money."

Even though I was taken aback that she had ignored my advice, I was impressed that she nailed a job at the Cooper House so soon after her arrival in Santa Cruz. Obviously her experience in retail back in Atlanta was paying off.

LYN WAS HIRED by Valerie Walden, who was five months pregnant and needed help managing her linen shop at the Cooper House. Valerie was married to Max Walden, a rotund, boisterous, white-haired man who reminded me of Santa Claus. When he laughed, which he did a lot, his belly actually jiggled.

Lyn excelled at her job. She, Max and Valerie became close friends, and Max quickly became her mentor. At times, Lyn and I were invited to the Waldens' home for dinner. I was starstruck at the thought of having dinner with the owners of the Cooper House when just weeks before I had been dancing with hippies on the sidewalk. After a while, Max encouraged Lyn to open her own store in the Cooper House. He recognized the potential she already showed at twenty-four.

Our mother saw that potential too. She was the one who suggested that Lyn open a franchise of i natural cosmetics, the makeup studio that she had first seen at Lenox Square

Mall in Atlanta. Mom also co-signed a small-business loan to get her started. Around the same time that Lyn joined me in Santa Cruz, Mom and Bill separated, and in 1977, Mom took a leave of absence from her job at the Centers for Disease Control in Atlanta and came to Santa Cruz to help Lyn launch her new cosmetics business. We three "girls" moved into an apartment together along with our mom's standard poodle, Jolie, who had come all the way from Atlanta with her.

Little did we know that Lyn was pioneering a family business. I had recently found myself at a dead end when, pursuing my dreams to become a dancer, I auditioned for the University of California Santa Cruz Performing Arts Department and was rejected. Lyn was right there, offering me a new beginning as assistant manager of her shop. I shaved my legs, started wearing makeup and commenced my new, unexpected aspiration: working in the Cooper House.

Mom was also there for us, working beside her daughters, adding words of encouragement and helpful ideas to promote the business. That summer the tourists were three deep around our cosmetic tables. Calmly and expertly, Lyn, Mom and I demonstrated cucumber facials and how to use our creamy café mocha eye shadow to create a more dramatic nighttime look.

As the summer season came to a close, Mom felt that we were well established in the new business and decided it was time for her to get back to Atlanta.

Lyn and I were having the time of our lives. We were young, single, attractive business owners. We would close up shop and kick off our night downstairs at the Cooper House

Lyn and me, with Noreen, an employee, at i natural cosmetics in the Cooper House.

Oak Room Saloon, a lively drinking spot with a massive carved oak bar and antique stained glass windows. We'd continue our party at Lulu Carpenters, another bar just a short walk down Pacific Garden Mall. We were both dating musicians in the popular band the Artichoke Brothers, better known as "The Chokes," so we often partied where they jammed at the Crow's Nest, the Catalyst and the Edge Water Bar in Capitola.

We had each other, and we had a successful business together. Lyn and I were compatible and in sync. That was new, and it felt good.

12

Busted

One morning in the fall of 1978, when we'd been running i natural cosmetics for a little more than a year, we were sipping coffee in the kitchen of our rented cliffside house at Sunset Beach. Lyn seemed preoccupied. Suddenly she said, "Dad called. He's coming here to see us."

My shoulders hunched up toward my ears and locked. Since my return from Colombia, Dad had been in touch more often, especially since his two-both were together. Lyn and I had long suspected that he was smuggling drugs. So many things about his life pointed that way. Lyn didn't tell me until she had moved to Santa Cruz, but when she was living in Las Vegas with Joyce, the FBI showed up one day. They were looking for Dad in conjunction with drug-trafficking charges.

Now, apparently, he believed that he could travel freely back to the United States. I was stunned. And a little bit frightened. "Don't you think it's dangerous for him to come here?" I said.

"I asked him that," Lyn replied. "He just told me that he really wants to see us and the new store. He says he misses us. You know Dad. He's going to do what he's going to do."

She was right. If Dad wasn't worried, I had to get over my concerns about the dangers he might face by coming to see us. I just decided in my mind that everything would work out. I pulled my shoulders back into place and said, "Come on, let's go. We only have thirty minutes to get to the shop."

A WEEK LATER, Dad waltzed into the Cooper House with a huge smile on his face. He was wearing a light-blue tailored suit with a white shirt unbuttoned at the neck. As usual, he looked handsome, fit and much younger than a man of almost fifty.

Lyn and I rushed over to him.

"My girls!" he exclaimed, hugging the two of us at the same time. After the excited embrace, he looked around the shop and said, "I'm so proud of you both. Lyn, I can't believe you did all of this."

Beaming, Lyn filled him in on how she had created the product displays, and how sales were going. When Lyn proudly led him down the hall to Max's office, Dad held my hand every step of the way.

"Max, this is my dad, Harold. He's visiting with us for a couple of days."

"Glad to meet you, Harold," Max roared as he reached out to shake hands with our dad. "Your girl is quite the business-woman. We are very pleased to have her here at the Cooper House. Make yourself at home. Have a drink at the bar or eat at the restaurant on me."

Dad thanked him, and Lyn and I took Dad around and introduced him to some of the other merchants, people who would remain our friends for decades: Clancy, who owned the Era women's clothing boutique, and Babette, owner of the Rainbow's End gift store.

The next afternoon at the Cooper House patio café, Dad placed two small velvet jewelry boxes on the table, one in front of Lyn and the other in front of me. He leaned toward us. "I love you girls so much," he said. "I miss you. You're all I live for."

I searched inside myself for the kind of love I had felt for him when I was a child, innocent and open. Yes, I was excited to see him that first day, but I had difficulty understanding how he could love me when we were so far apart in every way. Did he know me? Did he really want to know me? How could he love me if he didn't know me? I understood how my mom loved me: she supported my development and success in the world by teaching me ethics, the value of hard work, the importance of striving to achieve in school and the ability to make choices that fostered positive relationships. It was so much harder with my dad.

I couldn't tell him how I really felt. I wasn't even clear about that myself, or why I felt the way I did. I now realize that when I was in my twenties, I was too young and inexperienced to know my truth. I was still tormented by the untrue story that I had to please my father and be his baby girl in order to be loved by him. Yes, I was growing into a place of comfort within myself. Slowly but surely I was finding my voice. But somehow, when it came to my father, I was still not able to speak up.

I took a deep breath and tried to let myself feel my daddy's love. I so wanted to believe him. I still have the necklace he gave me that day, a Star of David stamped onto a gold medallion, with the words *Jeri* and *Daddy* engraved on the back. But as I stared at him across the table, I found myself shutting down inside. I faked a smile, pushed myself up from my chair, turned around and said, "Put it on me, Daddy."

THE NEXT MORNING, while I stayed at the shop, Lyn and Dad went out together to have breakfast at Aldo's, a small outdoor restaurant near the yacht harbor. An hour later Lyn burst through the door alone, tears cascading down her red, splotched face.

"Lyn, what's the matter?" I asked in a panic.

"Dad was arrested!" she sobbed.

In that moment, the fear I had pushed down when I heard Dad was coming to see us broke loose and burned in my chest.

I helped her, still crying, to a chair.

"We were in the car, almost at Aldo's," she told me, "when a whole bunch of cop cars surrounded us. A voice came over their loudspeaker telling us to stop the car and get out with our hands up.

"Dad pushed me to the floor and yelled, 'Okay, we're coming. We're coming out. I'm here with my daughter. Don't shoot!'"

She struggled to get her words out. I brought her some water and waited for her to calm down. At last she went on. "We got out and spread our arms on the side of the car. All of these cops, there must have been ten of them, were around us with their guns out. They handcuffed Dad and took him away in the back of a police car. They told me that I could go and just left me there standing in the street." She took a deep breath.

"It's my fault," Lyn said, wiping her face with a tissue.

"Lyn, it's not your fault. Why would you say that?" I asked, surprised.

She looked at me with puffy eyes. "Because before you got to the shop, he said something to me. I think he was trying to give me advice about the business, but I thought he was being critical of me. I don't know. It was his tone of voice I guess. I just felt like somehow I disappointed him. When he saw how upset I was, he apologized and told me that we could talk riding around in the car."

My sister was obviously just as dependent as I was on how my dad responded to her, and in her desire to please him.

I leaned over and held her. "Lyn, it's not your fault. I'm sure they could have arrested him almost anywhere the whole time he was here."

We agreed not to tell anyone at the Cooper House what had happened.

Later that morning we learned that our father had been taken to the Santa Cruz County Jail, right behind the Cooper House. Sometimes when I walked through the alley to my car after work, the prisoners in the fenced area on top of the building would wave and call out to me. The thought of Dad being one of those jailed men made me want to throw up.

Next morning, we called the jail first thing and were told that they had transported Dad to the San Francisco city jail, where they would hold him until the federal authorities could pick him up. They didn't know exactly when that was happening. On the chance that he would still be there, Lyn and I drove the seventy-five miles to San Francisco. I dreaded the thought of seeing my father in jail. Part of me hoped he would already be gone.

We waited in line with other visiting family members. After more than an hour, we were escorted through a couple of steel gates into a visiting room with glass partitions and telephone receivers. When Dad came out, we stared at him through the glass. My throat burned.

I couldn't touch him, and he couldn't touch me. My whole life, before this moment and since, Dad tried to cover up his fear, his sadness, any emotion or event that might hurt his daughters. He did the same thing that day. He smiled. He was neatly dressed in a brown prison uniform. But there was nothing he could do to avoid viewing his daughters through that glass partition as a proud man captured and detained by the police against his will.

He fidgeted with the phone cord, shifted in his seat and glanced down a lot as we talked. I could see he was agitated.

"Don't worry, my babies," he told us. "We'll get through this. I'm going to be okay. Don't worry. We'll be able to see each other again soon."

That night I took myself to the beach. I was alone. Like a wild, wounded horse, I ran as fast as I could under the full moon. When I was far away down the beach I screamed, just as I did that day in Miami: "Why does it have to be this way? I don't want it to be like this!! Why does my dad have to be a criminal?"

Something inside me was breaking apart. I didn't understand what it was exactly, but as much as I wanted that feeling of dread to go away, I suspected it never would. There was no escaping who my dad was, and I faced the very real possibility that this would not be the last time I'd have to go inside the grim confines of a prison to see him.

A MONTH LATER, just before Thanksgiving, Lyn and I found out that Dad had been moved from San Francisco to Florida and charged with narcotics trafficking. A couple of months after that, early in 1979, two agents showed up at the shop and asked if we knew where Dad was. They told us that after he was bailed out of jail in Florida to await his trial, he jumped bond. Now our dad was one of those people he used to track down when my sister and I were little girls living on Alverado Way, when he owned the bail bonding company he wanted us to inherit someday.

13

Tortured in Panama

After Dad jumped bail, things changed for Lyn and for me. Lyn decided to return to Atlanta to pursue her cosmetics career. She sold the shop, and I started dancing again.

Disco was all the rage in the late 1970s, especially after *Saturday Night Fever* came out. I asked Salvador, the Cooper House gardener, to take disco dance lessons with me. He showed up for our lessons decked out in his John Travolta boogie boots and tight bell-bottom jeans, chewing on a ginseng root that he told me gave him masculine energy and stamina. I was intrigued by Salvador's style and, yes, his masculine, well-shaped body, not to mention the deliciously sweet mangos he brought me after we started taking dance lessons.

Clancy, the owner of the women's clothing boutique, asked me to direct and choreograph a spring fashion show for the Era. The show was a huge success and catapulted me into my next career as the promotional and marketing director for the Cooper House. Salvador and I moved in together, and I was suddenly a mom, helping Salvador raise Chavo, his two-year-old son. Dad seemed far away, completely gone from my world. The golden engraved necklace he gave me lay hidden in a box deep in one of my dresser drawers.

Then one morning in June 1979, my phone rang. I was two months pregnant, living with Salvador in a small white house in a quiet neighborhood where I planned to have a home birth. I picked up the receiver and heard my sister's voice.

"Dad's in jail," she said. "He called to tell me that he was in a plane crash in Panama. They brought him back to the United States to stand trial for drug smuggling."

My breathing grew shallow. I searched my body for emotion, but it was as if all feeling had drained away, leaving an all-too-familiar numbness. I could hear the grief and fear in my sister's voice. Love welled up in me as I shifted my thoughts from my father to her.

"Are you okay, Lyn?" I asked.

She paused for a moment. "I'm relieved that no one was injured in the crash. They have Dad in the Miami-Dade federal prison, but they're transporting him here to Atlanta until his trial."

"Can you see him in Atlanta?"

"Probably. He said he would try to call me again."

"I wish I could be with you. Do you want me to try to come?"

"Oh, Ber, you don't need to do that. I'll call you when I know more."

"Please call me if you need anything, Lyn. I'm here for you. Tell Dad I love him."

Having my sister in my life to share worries about Dad was a godsend. We believed that no one else would understand what we, our father's daughters, were going through. We had one another to talk to, and while that was surely helpful, it still felt to me like we were isolated somewhere out at sea, on a small island all by ourselves.

At the time it never occurred to me to try to seek out organizations that assisted families that had an incarcerated parent. I likely wouldn't have found much support in the 1970s anyway. Fortunately there are programs and resources for family members and children with incarcerated parents today, although much more help is still needed. Recent studies show that on any given day in the United States there are 2.7 million children with an incarcerated parent, and four times that number have experienced parental incarceration in their lifetime.

Around 1997, Lyn asked Dad to explain what he did in South America and why he did what he did. We were both still grappling with questions about how our father got mixed up with a life of crime. He wrote several stories for us, including one about the plane crash in Panama.

The pilot, a couple of crew, Dad and one of his partners, Jorge Valdés, were flying in a twin-engine Beechcraft Queen Air plane from Colombia to Nicaragua with cocaine valued at four million dollars. At five thousand feet, flying at two hundred miles per hour, they lost both engines and crashed moments later in a small open field lined by thick banana trees.

Miraculously, the plane didn't burst into flames, and Dad and the others on board walked away with their lives.

When Manuel Noriega, then a colonel in the Panamanian army, ordered his men to search the crashed plane, they found the kilos of cocaine. My father and Jorge, who was only twenty-two at the time, were put in a jail cell and tortured in the bowels of la Cárcel Modelo, the vilest prison in Panama. This was my father's story about their torture by Leno, the man responsible for getting information out of prisoners:

> I was put in a chair with my hands cuffed in a painful position under the chair. I was beaten and then taken to the dungeon cell. It was an old Spanish fort from over 200 years ago when Spain ruled the land. I was stripped naked. Nothing was in the cell, just a dirty concrete floor and a pee can. I was kept handcuffed to the bars at all times. Leno's torture techniques were electric cattle prods, beatings, gasoline thrown on me, stand naked all day and hit if I moved much, but I didn't talk.

He went on to explain how he was able to survive such a brutal predicament.

> I conditioned myself for pain all my life. I beat myself with bunches of branches and squeezed my fingers and toes with pliers. Plus fighting [boxing] had conditioned me for pain. When I

> was in South America I would run through tall jungle grass that cut and hurt to condition my skin. I still try to keep myself conditioned by running barefoot summer and winter and just wearing shorts on cold days. I tumble and roll on the ground and have an obstacle course here for myself. I have a high threshold for pain and don't stop working out because of an injury.

He then wrote, "What do you think of your daddy now? He's pretty crazy, don't you think?"

I had to agree. He had never been a regular father, and he was crazy to do the wild and dangerous things he did.

During our visits to see Dad at United States Penitentiary (USP) Leavenworth, USP Coleman and USP Atlanta, he would tell Lyn and me about some of his adventures in the jungles, like crashing planes, being shot at as he ran from the Colombian military to escape capture, and cooling off in rain forest rivers populated with huge anacondas. As he spoke, he would smile at us, his eyes wide, as if reliving the danger was fun for him. He seemed to delight in the fact that he was not normal.

Dad's accomplice, Jorge Valdés, also wrote about their experiences in La Modelo. He published his version of the plane crash and capture in a book called *Coming Clean: The True Story of a Cocaine Drug Lord and His Unexpected Encounter with God*. His account matches and expands upon my father's. He describes terrible torture as the guards tried to extract information from both men, and he concludes the chapter "Tortured" with a shocking scene:

> "Don't let them defeat you, Jorge," Harold kept saying. "The harder you fight back, the easier it will be." In our underwear, Harold and I lay motionless on a concrete floor stained with a sticky mosaic of blood, excrement, and vomit ...
>
> Our torturers made a crucial mistake in allowing Harold and me to remain in the same cell. Had they separated us, one or both of us might have given up. But together, our power increased exponentially. Harold and I talked through the night. Occasionally, I'd glance over at him and just shake my head, amazed at his stamina. He was filthy and his body reeked with a horrible stench, but his spirit was that of a warrior. He had the heart of a giant. We were still alive, and we had given no information to the guards.

I was horrified to tears to read about my father being tortured, yet deeply moved to read that Jorge described my father as having the spirit of a warrior and the heart of a giant. Would Jorge have survived if my father were any other way? Would Dad have survived?

After four weeks of brutal torture, Dad and Jorge's ordeal in La Modelo finally showed signs of coming to an end. They were told they would be escorted to a plane that would take them to Costa Rica; instead, when they got to the airport, a platoon of soldiers streamed in and put them on a plane to Miami, where they were arrested and charged with conspiracy to bring narcotics into the United States.

Dad then spent eight months in solitary confinement in the Atlanta federal penitentiary while the government built a case against him.

In the meantime, Lyn was managing a prestigious skin care salon in the Atlanta area. Until early 1980, she visited Dad on her days off. Then he was moved to Macon, Georgia, for his trial. Joyce went to Macon for the trial, but Lyn couldn't take the time off work.

Before the trial began, Joyce asked Lyn to come to the courthouse in Macon to talk with Dad. His lawyers were saying they could get him a sentence of fifteen years through a plea bargain, but he had refused. If he went to trial, he would likely be sentenced to thirty years.

Distraught, Lyn was determined to get Dad to listen to her, to change his mind. Before she drove to see him, she wrote a letter, getting her argument straight and every point clear. When the attorneys took her in to see him, she burst into tears. "Dad, I'm going to read you this letter because I don't want to lose you," she sobbed. In the letter she told him how much she loved him and that she wanted him to do the right thing for his family. It worked. Dad took the plea bargain and received fifteen years.

He spent six more months in the Atlanta penitentiary. That fall he was transferred to a medium-security prison in Memphis, Tennessee, where we thought he would serve the remaining years of his sentence. Not even a year later, though, during his regular Sunday phone call with Lyn, he said a surprising thing: "I'll be seeing you soon." Lyn began to worry about what he might be planning.

A few days later a black Cadillac pulled up in front of the salon where Lyn worked. The door opened and Dad got out. She was terrified. As soon as he stepped inside the salon, she took his arm and walked him back to the car.

"What are you doing here?" she said, keeping her voice low. "This is the first place they're going to look for you!"

"I just couldn't stay there. I may go down, but I'm doing it my way," Dad said.

That was it. The conversation was over. He hugged her, got back in the car and left. Stunned, she stood in the parking lot for a long time. What had just happened? Clearly, Dad had escaped from prison. She should have called the police and reported his visit. But she never made that call.

Two days later a man named Wilbur came to the salon and told Lyn that he could take her to see Dad. She told Herb, her boyfriend who lived with her, that she had to go see him. Herb knew he couldn't talk her out of it, so he did what he could to protect her. He said he would go with her, and insisted that they follow in their own vehicle rather than ride in a car with Wilbur.

The next day Wilbur led them to Dobbins Air Force Base, where Herb stayed in the car and Wilbur took Lyn to a small building. When she stepped inside, she saw two men sitting at a table. One of them got up and walked over to a door, opened it and said, "Harold, your daughter's here." From what Lyn could tell, they had been hiding him in a closet. One of the men took Dad and Lyn for a drive so they could have some privacy to visit.

When I asked my sister why she would endanger herself to be with our dad, she said, "I know it was dangerous and broke the law, but I needed to see him to be reassured that he was okay."

Those brief moments gave her only fleeting reassurance. We never did figure out who was helping Dad, but they returned him to his drug-trafficking business in South America. And once he was there, days and weeks would go by without any of us hearing from him.

To THIS DAY, I don't believe my sister and I know the truth about how our father escaped from that prison in Memphis, but this is what he told us when we asked him:

> Uncle Al came to see me and asked me if I wanted to stay or get out. I immediately said, go. I knew I would be paroled in a couple more years but that was too long for me. I hated people telling me what to do. I had a serious problem adjusting to prison rules and the confines of a cell after being free in the jungles of South America.
>
> Arrangements were made to pay my way out of Memphis. During the month of October 1981 my own clothes were brought to me. At approximately 7:00 pm on October 27, a guard escorted me to a storage area where I changed clothes. I was given a prison guard badge and told to walk to the front gate between 8:00 and 8:20. I walked right out of the prison and into a car that was waiting for me.

> I was taken to the airport and given a ticket to Atlanta. A friend picked me up at the Atlanta airport and drove me to Dobbins Air Force Base where I stayed for about three weeks while transportation was arranged to take me to South America. While I was waiting at Dobbins Air Force Base I was introduced to a retired major, Loy Shipp, who told me he wanted to fly drug smuggling planes to Colombia. He also showed a strong interest in my affiliations with the guerrillas. He knew I was affiliated with the M-19 in Colombia, a guerrilla organization that has been trying to overthrow the Colombian government for years.

When I read his story, I was even more confused. Who was Uncle Al? Who paid to get Dad out and why? How could an escaped inmate be held on a U.S. military base? Was Dad used by the Drug Enforcement Administration (DEA) and Central Intelligence Agency (CIA) to lead them to bigger players in the smuggling cartels, men like Pablo Escobar? When I asked Dad these questions, his answers didn't help much. I wondered if he didn't want me to know the answers, or if he actually didn't know himself.

14

Fugitive Father

Letters from Dad were rare, but it just so happened that Lyn was visiting me in Santa Cruz when I received one in January 1982. My son, Sol, was two years old at the time.

> *Two-both,*
>
> *I've been thinking about you girls. Sol must be so cute now. The Ber has her hands full with him. I want to see him. Now she knows what I went through with two-both. It was my lucky day when I got you girls. So when we get the money, the Ber can come here for a short vacation.*
>
> *From your daddy*

I wrote back to the address that he had told me to use:

Hi Dad.

Just opened your letter. Little Sol is so good. Having him makes me remember when we were a family living on Alverado Way. I can't believe you're a grandpa! I'm enclosing some photos. I hope you are okay.

Love, the Ber, Sol, Sal and Chavo

Feb 24 1982

To my Mommy Ber and my Beautiful Daughter

Hi Honey,

Just got your letters today and pics. Our family. Honey, I want to see you so much. Your letters bring tears to my eyes, a lump in my throat and an ache in my heart. What is life if I can't be with my loved ones? I want you to be safe. Don't be afraid or scared. When you come for a visit all will be arranged. I'll be working in the next week or two and we will have the money we need. I'm going to Bolivia to put together a deal. So keep your fingers crossed.

You sure make me a proud and happy dad.

Considering everything I had been through with our dad, it was beyond any logic, but I continued to want to have a relationship with him. Now that I had my own children, Sol and Chavo, I felt closer to my dad and really wanted him to see his grandkids. I had a familial bond that most people would consider insane based on the circumstances.

In mid-October 1982, a year after Dad escaped, I opened my mailbox on Pryce Street and reached in to find another letter from him. In this one he gave a specific day and time that he would call me at a payphone down the street from my house. So on a foggy evening I walked out my door, turned right onto Ocean Street and stood waiting for his call at the payphone next to Ferrell's Donut Shop.

The sky spread purple above me. I watched the breeze pick up a discarded paper coffee cup on the sidewalk and toss it into the air. Ten minutes passed, then fifteen. I shivered and pulled my sweater tighter around me. Had something happened? Like my sister, I worried about Dad when I didn't hear from him. I lowered my head and turned to walk home, but had taken only a few steps when the phone rang. I bolted back and grabbed the receiver.

"Hello!"

"Ber!" My father's strong, confident voice boomed through the receiver.

"Dad! Happy birthday, Dad! You're sure getting up there." Dad's fifty-first birthday was a few days away, on October 20. "Have you been using black shoe polish on your gray hair?" I asked him, laughing over the phone.

Years earlier, when I was ten and he was in prison for the first time, I had written, *Dear Pop, are you getting any older? If so there's always black shoe polish to cover up the gray hair!!* Ever since, I had been teasing him about using shoe polish to keep looking young.

He chuckled. "Yes, I have, and it works really good." His voice softened. "How are you doing, Ber? I really miss you."

My heart fluttered. I tried to change the subject. "Everything's good here, Dad," I said. "The boys keep me really busy."

He continued in his somber, tender voice. "Look, honey, I'll wire money for you and the kids to come here. I would really love to see you."

Goose bumps spread over my arms. I imagined seeing him pick up Sol and throw him in the air like he used to do with me when I was a little girl. I leaned in and mumbled, "Okay, Dad. Let me talk it over with Salvador. I would really love to see you too."

"Just let me know what day and time you'll be here," he said, as if he had no doubts that I would come. "The best place to fly into is Bogotá. From there we can go together to my house in Medellín."

It was amazing how Dad could make flying with two small children almost four thousand miles to an unfamiliar country at the heart of international drug smuggling seem like walking across the street to have lunch at Denny's. Yet my yearning to be with him was concealing the reality of just how dangerous it was to be with my father. I closed my eyes, took a long, shuddering breath and heard myself say, "Okay, Dad."

As if the plans were now firm, he told me to write down a phone number to call if something went wrong. "It will be fine. I promise. Nothing's going to happen. I'll be waiting for you at the airport in Bogotá. Just send the flight information to that address I gave you. Bye, sweetheart. I can't wait to see you! Oh, and I'm really excited for you to meet Veronika. She's really nice. Love you, Ber."

Veronika was Dad's new German girlfriend, whom he had met in the Bahamas. Dad and Joyce were now divorced.

"Bye, Dad," I said and heard a click at his end. I wiped my eyes, hung up the receiver and walked home in a blur. My mind raced. Colombia! Was I really going to go back there? With my children? Against all reason, I knew I was going to try.

The next day, I was in the kitchen making breakfast when the phone rang. It was Mom, who called every Sunday morning. I told her that Dad had asked me to visit him.

"Jeri, I'm really worried about you going to Colombia. I know you want to see your dad." She paused. "But anything could happen in such a dangerous place."

I held the receiver between my cheek and shoulder while I mixed pancake batter with both hands. Chavo and Sol were chasing each other around the kitchen. Salvador was out for a run.

"But, Mom, I want Dad to meet my kids. He really wants me to come. He misses me."

"You don't know what you're getting yourself into, Jeri. Your dad is a fugitive. You need to be realistic."

I blanked out her words of caution because I believed I had no choice. If I were realistic and practical when it came to my dad, I wouldn't have a relationship with him. That was not an option for me.

Behind me, dining room chairs screeched across the kitchen floor toward the hot stove.

"I have to go, Mom," I said hastily. "I'll call you later."

That evening, when I told Salvador that Dad wanted us to visit him in Colombia, he agreed readily. I wasn't surprised.

He knew how much I cared for my dad, and he, like me, was proud of the family we had created together. He was willing to help me, to help us visit Dad. I felt much better knowing that he—a fluent Spanish speaker and a supportive partner—would be with us.

We decided to go first to Salvador's hometown, Los Reyes in the state of Michoacán, Mexico. We would purchase our tickets to Bogotá in Mexico City, hopefully throwing anyone who might try to follow us off our trail.

Two months later, on January 4, 1983, we landed in Guadalajara, rented a white Chevrolet Impala and drove four hours to the small town of Los Reyes. For six days we ate, slept and explored, enjoying the tranquil streets and the hospitality of Salvador's family. When it was time to leave for Mexico City, I felt a flicker of panic watching their waving arms get smaller and smaller as we drove away down the dusty, narrow street. All my thoughts about the dangers of going to Colombia flooded back, breaking through my denial. Just how dangerous would it be to visit Dad there? Would we be kidnapped or robbed, or would we be with him when the Colombian police surrounded our car with their guns drawn, like the police did in Santa Cruz? Within just twenty-four hours we would be touching down at Bogotá's El Dorado International Airport. There was no turning back.

"GIVE ME YOUR HAND and stay with me," I told three-year-old Sol as we collected our luggage and made our way through

Customs and Immigration. At least we all have passports, I thought briefly, unlike me so many years ago.

We came out of customs into the reception area where Dad had said he would meet us. I looked behind me to be sure Chavo was still with Salvador. We cut through a crowd of strangers, boldly gesturing as they spoke rapid Spanish. My heart raced.

Any moment I would be hugging my father.

My eyes darted from person to person, searching for Dad's familiar face. I didn't see him. Ten minutes later I was still standing there. I didn't realize how hard I was clutching Sol's hand until he let out a yelp. "Ouch, Mommy."

"He'll be here," I said to Salvador. "He's just running late." I pointed to some empty chairs. Sol climbed into the chair next to me and rummaged through my backpack.

"Mommy, read me this," he said moments later, holding out *Where the Wild Things Are*.

"Just look at the pictures, Sol," I told him, still searching the crowds and growing more and more frightened. What if Dad had been captured and was unable to meet us? What would we do if he never came?

Salvador's voice interrupted my anxious thoughts. "Chavo has to pee. We're going to look for a bathroom." I watched them walk away hand in hand.

TWENTY MINUTES LATER we were still waiting. Salvador was trying to convince me that we should start thinking about where to stay. It was getting late, long past the boys' bedtime.

"But Dad told us to wait here," I said. Surely Dad would come running up to us at any minute.

"Jeri, we need a place to sleep," Salvador insisted.

At last I gave up.

Outside, in the warm and humid night air, taxi drivers swarmed us like mosquitos. "Señor! Señor! Taxi, taxi!" they shouted as we huddled together on the sidewalk. Salvador motioned to one of them.

The driver hurried over to us, grabbed a suitcase in each hand, tossed them into the trunk of his beat-up black cab and whisked us off through the loud, bustling nighttime streets of Bogotá.

Fifteen minutes later we arrived at a rundown hotel that we were pretty sure paid off taxi drivers who brought unsuspecting visitors to their door. Wanting to get settled somewhere, anywhere, we checked in and lugged our suitcases down a narrow hallway to the elevator. Salvador got the door to our room open after jiggling the key several times. When we stepped inside, we were greeted by the rank smell of stale cigarette smoke.

"What have we gotten ourselves into?" I said wearily.

"It'll be okay, Jeri," Sal told me. "Don't worry. Let's just get the boys to bed."

He wheeled in our suitcases as I collapsed on the bed that took up most of the room.

Chavo crawled over to me and asked, "Where's Grandpa?"

Startled by his innocent question, I felt my eyes fill with tears. "He's coming," I whispered, turning my face away, not sure of anything.

"I'll stay here with the kids while you go make that phone call," Salvador said when he saw me wiping tears from my eyes.

I found the piece of paper with the number Dad had given me and took the elevator back to the lobby. The clerk took the paper from my shaking hand as I explained to him that I needed his help to make a phone call. He dialed the number and handed me the receiver. I listened to every ring, hardly breathing. Then a click and a man's voice: "*Bueno.*"

"Hello! Hello!" I stammered, gripping the receiver. "This is Jeri. Harold Rosenthal's daughter. Please give my father the name of this hotel and tell him to come. We are waiting for him here."

He replied in Spanish. I hung up, not even thinking to ask the clerk to translate for me. Nor had I thought to ask Salvador to make the call. I let out a frustrated sigh and headed back to the elevator. I had no idea if the man who answered even knew what I was saying.

An hour later, the boys and Salvador had fallen asleep fully clothed on top of the bedspread. I lay down next to them. I must have fallen into an exhausted doze, because the knock startled me. I jerked up from the bed, stumbled to the door and cracked it open ever so slightly.

Standing in the dimly lit hallway was my father.

"Dad!" I shouted, swinging the door open wide.

He stepped in and wrapped his arms around me. As I nestled into his comforting warmth, all my fears and doubts slipped away.

"Ber, I'm so sorry. I got held up. I got here as quickly as I could. Are you okay?" he asked, pushing my bangs off my forehead and looking straight into my eyes.

"Dad, I'm so glad to see you! I was so scared that something had happened to you."

"I know, I know. It's okay now. I'm here."

Together we looked over at the bed, where the boys were just waking up. Salvador was standing, clearly waiting to be introduced.

"Dad, this is Salvador. You met him once a few years ago at the Cooper House."

Salvador held out his hand.

Dad shook it vigorously, his smile welcoming. "Hey, Sal," he said. "Thanks so much for bringing the kids and Jeri here to see me."

"This is Chavo and this is Sol," I said, nodding toward the boys, who were staring at us sleepily. "Your grandkids."

"I can't believe I'm a grandpa," he replied, laughing. "Is that true? Is that true? Look." He leaned forward and showed the bewildered boys the top of his head. "I don't have gray hair. I'm not old enough to be a grandpa."

Within minutes, Dad was hugging the boys. He reached an arm around Sol's waist, picked him up and held him like he used to do with my sister and me when we were kids. A smile broke out across my tired face.

"Oh, oh. You're heavy," he stammered, leaning and putting him back down on the floor. Then, "You must be hungry. Let's get out of here," he said, grabbing a suitcase in each hand. "This place is a dump."

We all got into a taxi that took us nonstop to the Bogotá Hilton. I finally felt the knot in my shoulders relax.

The next morning we boarded a small plane, flew over the dense jungle canopy for almost an hour and dropped precariously onto a small landing strip nestled among the peaks of the Andes.

Veronika greeted us wearing a colorful sleeveless cotton blouse and a form-fitting mid-calf white skirt that accented her slim, tanned body. Her wrists were covered with silver bracelets that jangled when she reached over to hug me. Like me, she wore little makeup and had her light-brown hair pulled back in a ponytail.

"Jeri, I heard so much about you," she said in her thick German accent with a big, friendly smile. "We wait for you to come for some time now. These your boys? Oh, how cute they are. And this must be your husband."

She was warm and welcoming.

After our suitcases were safely tucked into the trunk of the car, Salvador and I climbed into the back seat and pulled the boys onto our laps. I was surprised when Veronika jumped behind the wheel and Dad opened the passenger door and got in. Once we were underway, she shouted back at us, "We don't let Harold drive here."

An image flashed into my mind of Dad being stopped for a traffic violation, asked to get out of the car and then being pushed down on the car and handcuffed. I didn't want to think about the consequences if that happened here, in a foreign country so far away from home.

"Look, Palé!" Chavo shouted, using his word for his daddy,

having never learned to say *padre*. He was pointing out the window at a horse pulling a wooden wagon loaded with straw. His outburst snapped me out of my fearful thoughts. I exhaled and sat back in my seat.

Veronika maneuvered the car through crowded streets. Medellín was more modern than I expected. Skyscrapers towered over us, and men in business suits and women in high heels strode along the sidewalks, passing colorfully dressed Indian villagers who had come down from the mountains to sell their wares. Dad and Veronika talked in the front seat while we stared out the windows on either side.

Leaving the city behind, we drove for about twenty minutes up winding mountain roads and pulled into a driveway cut through the dense tropical jungle that surrounded Dad and Veronika's home. This turned out to be a relatively modest three-bedroom house with a large living room, built on the side of a mountain overlooking the cocaine capital of the world.

"We're here!" Veronika exclaimed.

As we climbed out of the car, two women emerged from the house to help us with our luggage. I realized they were housekeepers.

"*Bienvenidos*," they exclaimed, smiling as they took one suitcase each and escorted us to what was to be our room for the next week.

Lunch was ready. We were sitting together for the first time as a family, talking about our time in Mexico, when a knock interrupted us. Dad got up and opened the door to reveal a tall dark man standing outside. He waved his arms at

Dad emphatically and spoke low and fast. Dad replied calmly, also in a voice too quiet for us to hear.

After a minute, Dad turned to us. "I have to take care of a few things, Ber," he told me. "Veronika can show you and the kids the monkeys. I'll be back in a little while."

"Oh yes, yes!" Veronika said, pointing out toward the yard. "Come with me. They are just outside there."

After playing with the monkeys and pushing the boys in the hammock, we went back inside to our room to read and rest. The boys fell asleep. Veronika left to run some errands. Two hours later I heard the front door close and recognized my father's voice.

"Dad's back," I said to Salvador. "I'll go out and talk to him."

When I got to the living room, Dad was standing there with another man, not the one who had come to the door earlier. This man was an American.

"Jeri, this is Loy Shipp. He's one of my pilots. Boy, he could tell you some crazy stories," Dad said with that low chuckle of his.

Loy put out his hand to shake mine. "Hello, Jeri. Welcome to Colombia."

Dad interjected. "As soon as Veronika gets back, we're going with Loy over to some friends' for dinner. I want them to meet you."

"What about Salvador and the kids?" I asked.

"Oh, the maid will make them something to eat. It would be better if you came alone."

Reluctantly I agreed.

Forty-five minutes later, Veronika pulled our car into a circular driveway and parked in front of an opulent Spanish-style mansion.

An attractive golden-haired woman in a low-cut red crocheted blouse greeted us at the door. "Harold, *vente*," she said. "Come in. *Esta es su hija*, your daughter from California?"

"*Si, si*," he answered.

I shook hands with her and was ushered into the dining room, where more people were laughing and talking in Spanish. When they saw us, one of the men stood up. "*Hola*, Harold. *Siéntate*," he said, his voice boisterous.

Dad put his arm around me and pulled me forward. His pride was obvious. "This is my daughter Jeri. She came all the way from California to be with me."

"*Bueno, bueno, mucho gusto*," the man said, motioning us to sit down. Dad sat next to me while we waited to be served a traditional Colombian dish, *ajiaco*, a soup made with chicken, potatoes and cream. I ate quietly. Dad talked mostly to Loy, who was sitting across from us.

An hour passed. By now my father and Loy had left the dinner table to talk in an adjoining room with some other men. I was ready to go, but I sat patiently, waiting. Dad finally came to me, leaned over and kissed the top of my head.

"I have to leave for a while to do some business, Ber. Veronika will give you a ride," he said. And with that he left me in a house of strangers.

I was exhausted and asked if I could lie down somewhere until Veronika was ready to leave. One of the women who had served us dinner ushered me down the hall, into a room that looked like a den or study. I lay down on a brown leather couch and fell asleep almost instantly.

When I woke, I felt sick and disoriented and had no idea how much time had passed. I straightened my clothes and hair as best I could and went back out to the dining room, only to find that Veronika was gone. She had forgotten about me. One of the men I was introduced to earlier had to give me a ride back to my dad's house.

The next day Dad had us pile in the car, with Veronika driving, to check out the nearby mountain vistas. We stopped to get a bite to eat along the way. I could tell the boys and Salvador were enjoying themselves. Yet Dad seemed distant to me, preoccupied. Of course, they wouldn't have known that, having just met him.

As soon as we got back to the house, Loy Shipp whisked Dad away to another business meeting. The upbeat mood with which he greeted us on that first day had vanished, and it was clear to me that he really didn't have time to spend with us. I regretted making the effort to bring my family to visit. However, I did my best to keep things on an even keel now that we were four thousand miles from home. I stuffed my disappointment deep inside and smiled when, on the third day, Dad gave us the keys to his car so we could explore the town on our own. Without him, we went to the zoo and local parks and restaurants. Veronika left that same day on a trip to the United States. I never saw her again.

The day before we flew back to California, Dad called me into his office. I stood by the window, watching as he half leaned, half sat on his rustic wooden desk. He knitted his brows and looked at me, then waved his hand over a bunch of lined yellow legal tablets filled with handwritten notes.

"Jeri," he said, "you are part of the family business. All of this belongs to you and Lyn."

My body went numb. Was he asking me to be involved in drug smuggling? All I could do was nod silently, as I always did with Dad. I closed my eyes to escape the thought that my own father would consider involving his beloved daughter in such a violent, dangerous business. When I opened them, I was looking at a man I barely recognized. The conversation ended there. Perhaps he saw my reluctance, despite the nod of my head. I don't know.

As we pulled into the airport the next day with Dad and his driver, the late afternoon sun had dipped behind the Andes. The kids and Salvador went around the car to get our bags from the trunk, leaving Dad and me alone near the front of the car. He put his arms around my shoulders. I looked over at him and burst out crying. Alarmed, he stepped back and stared at me with a pained face.

"Ber, what is it? What is it? Why are you crying?" he exclaimed, clearly exasperated.

I couldn't speak through my trembling gasps. Anyway, what could I say?

"It's okay. It's going to be okay," he said, hugging me close.

Sure, Dad, I thought. That's what you always say.

I wanted to shout at him, to tell him it was not okay. Instead I took a deep breath and lied, same as always. "I know, Dad," I told him. "It's going to be okay. Take care of yourself, Dad."

He held my hand until we had to part at the gate. I followed Salvador and the boys up the metal stairs onto the plane. When I got to the top of the stairs, I turned to wave my last goodbye and saw Dad standing at the window in the airport, waving back. I could read his lips saying, "I love you."

With those words, an unexpected sadness swept over me, the same sense of dread that engulfed me the first time I saw my father in the San Francisco jail. I wanted things to be different with him. I wanted my dad to be with me and my family. Instead he was a fugitive in a far-off country, running from the law.

I turned and went inside the plane. As I sat down beside Salvador, I was overwhelmed by an unshakable feeling that something tragic was going to happen to my father. As our plane took flight away from Colombia, I knew that no matter how hard I tried to deny the reality of my father's life, it was not going to be okay.

EIGHT MONTHS LATER, Dad and his driver were sitting at a traffic light in Bogotá. The DEA and Colombian police surrounded his car with their guns drawn. He was captured without a struggle and soon afterward extradited to the United States to stand trial as a drug-trafficking kingpin. The day I boarded that plane in Medellín with my family was the last time I ever saw my father a free man.

As it turned out, I didn't have to worry about drug enforcement agencies tailing us to find Dad. Loy Shipp, the pilot we met at his house, was working for the CIA, and several other men that Dad employed were undercover DEA agents. They had likely been following him since his escape in Memphis, long before I set foot in Colombia and had dinner with the Medellín cartel.

15

Life Sentence

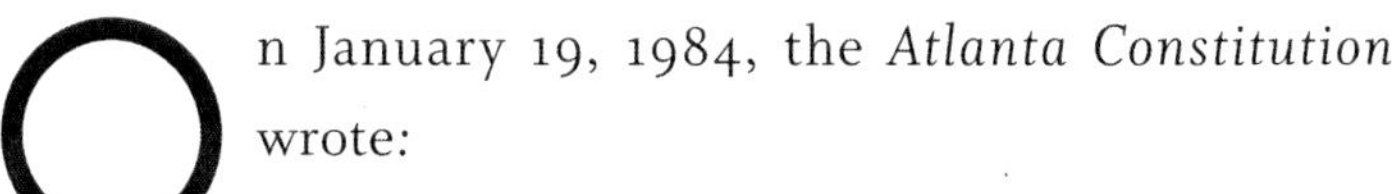

On January 19, 1984, the *Atlanta Constitution* wrote:

> Thirty people have been indicted in the "largest cocaine trafficking ring in the nation's history," authorities announced Monday. Associate U.S. Attorney General D. Lowell Jensen said the ring smuggled about 5 tons of cocaine worth $940 million from Colombia into Georgia, Florida, Tennessee, and Pennsylvania between June 1982 and September 1983. The Atlanta indictment identified Harold J. Rosenthal, 53, as the ring-leader of the cocaine operation.

Dad was once again held in solitary confinement at USP Atlanta as the prosecution built its case.

My sister didn't attend the four-month jury trial. Her attorney advised her against it. While Dad was in Colombia awaiting extradition, three DEA agents showed up at Lyn's apartment. They wanted to know if she had ever contacted people on Dad's behalf to accept money or drugs. She told them she hadn't, but they indicted her anyway.

A month later she spent a day anxiously waiting in the hallway of the courthouse while her attorney met with the U.S. prosecuting attorney, Craig Gillen. In the end, she agreed not to help Dad in any way with communication to outside people during his trial, and was offered a guarantee that she would not have to testify in his case. The indictment against her was dropped.

On November 26, 1984, our father was found guilty and sentenced to life in prison without the possibility of parole, fined $425,000, and given sentences totaling 180 years on one count of racketeering under the Racketeer Influenced and Corrupt Organizations Act (RICO); one count of engaging in a continuing criminal enterprise (CCE); and seven counts of importing cocaine into the United States. The CCE alone was referred to as a "living-death" or "pine-box" sentence because the offender is ineligible for release while alive. Dad was handcuffed, led out of the courtroom and transported to Marion, the federal super-max prison in Illinois, where he was put in solitary confinement for four years.

At the end of the trial, Lyn called to tell me that Dad had been sentenced to life without parole. The finality of his sentence—that he would be in prison for the rest of his life—didn't seem real to me. I didn't want to believe that Dad would be in prison for the rest of his life. He'd get out, I thought, just like he always did.

When Dad wrote, years later, about his experiences in South America, I learned that in addition to smuggling cocaine he was trafficking arms to the Revolutionary Armed Forces of Colombia (FARC), that country's largest left-wing rebel group. FARC was established in 1964 as the armed wing of the Communist Party, upholding a Marxist–Leninist ideology. The group's main founders were small farmers and land workers who had banded together to fight against the staggering levels of inequality and oppression in Colombia at the time.

From about 1975 until his capture in 1983, Dad not only supplied the guerrillas of FARC and the M-19 (another revolutionary group that had been trying to overthrow the Colombian government for years) with arms and cocaine money, but he also became one of them. In 1979, the same year his plane carrying cocaine to Nicaragua crashed in a banana plantation in Panama, he was being hunted by the Colombian government and labeled a dangerous "Gringo Guerrilla" in local papers and news broadcasts.

In the transcripts of his trial, where he testified in his own defense, Dad stated, "I have spent a lot of time in these third world countries. I saw a lot of killings. Useless killing. Slaughtering of people, little kids getting machine-gunned in the streets by the government forces in Colombia.

I was inflamed over it. If you saw this killing, the murders and atrocities in these countries, maybe you would be changed. And I was. I was very moved by it and that's what I stand on and that's what I did, Mr. Gillen."

Craig Gillen then asked him, "Are you now, and have [you] been for a majority of your adult life, a Marxist communist?"

Dad replied, "When you say communist and Marxist, I think you need to separate them. Do you want an explanation?"

"Well, why don't you tell us what you are?"

"I think that's a broad question, Mr. Gillen."

"Well, are you a communist?"

"No," Dad answered.

"Are you a Marxist?"

"I have that philosophy and that belief."

Craig Gillen asked, "Well I take it on the purpose of our direct examination that is the reason why you had these communist friends and affiliations down in South America. Isn't that correct?"

"Yes," Dad replied.

We won't ever know for sure, but when I read what Dad wrote about his dealings in South America that included supplying arms to the guerrillas, I began to suspect that he became a person of interest to the CIA when they found out that he had affiliations with FARC, the M-19 and the Sandinistas in Nicaragua. At the time, the United States government was pouring millions of dollars into Colombia to fight FARC and the Sandinistas. Our father was right there on the battlefields of the Cold War between the superpowers, the Soviet Union and the United States.

Dad wrote:

> During the late 1970s and early 1980s cocaine was valued at $40,000 a kilo at the wholesale price in Miami. The Colombian peso had no value outside the country. That meant that only the U.S. dollar could be used to purchase arms, ammo, and other necessary supplies for the revolutionary guerrillas. The leftist guerrillas used drugs to fund their revolutionary wars. Cocaine became a cash revenue for the guerrillas and they were working with the cocaine cartels. The left and the right both used drugs to finance their wars.

In other words, not only were left-wing terrorist groups like FARC and the M-19 using money from drug smuggling to fund their efforts to overthrow the Colombian government, but the right-wing, U.S.-backed terrorist Contras in Nicaragua were as well. As the result of an investigation by Senator John Kerry and the Senate Foreign Relations Committee, it is now well known that in 1986 the U.S. State Department made payments to Contras involved in drug trafficking.

In 1981, after Dad escaped from the Memphis federal prison, Loy Shipp paid him a visit at Dobbins Air Force Base. Dad had no idea that Shipp had worked in the National Security Agency (NSA) when George H.W. Bush was head of the CIA. The two of them talked about the Colombian guerrillas and Communists in South America and their subversive revolutionary wars. Shipp told Dad that he wanted to fly drugs.

According to Dad's written accounts, Loy Shipp made trips to Colombia, bringing U.S. Air Force aeronautical charts and other military documents in order to brief traffickers on U.S. defense zones and how to evade capture. Cartel traffickers that Dad referred to as "Los Pablos" flew Loy Shipp to various jungle air strips, learning from the expertise Shipp had gained while flying and landing in the jungles of Vietnam.

I believe Dad was a pawn in a much bigger game, which he may or may not have known about. I also believe that his arrest in Colombia saved his life. Right after he was arrested and returned to the United States, the reign of terror instigated by Pablo Escobar, the Medellín cartel's drug lord, escalated. When Escobar was associated with planning the assassination of Justice Minister Lara in 1984, the year my father was put in prison for life, the Colombian state began its first serious offensive against the Medellín cartel.

Over the next ten years, until Escobar was killed in 1993, Bogotá and Medellín experienced atrocious violence. Car bombs killed innocent people. Government buildings were attacked, including a violent siege of the Colombian Supreme Court that took the lives of twelve of the justices.

At the time, I thought that Dad's life sentence took him away from my family and from me, but eventually I realized that his capture and resulting incarceration gave him back to us. Dad said many times over the years that if he hadn't been caught and put in prison, he would be dead.

Over the years of Dad's incarceration, he told my sister and me a time or two that what he did—trafficking drugs—was wrong. I don't know how much remorse he felt or exactly how he meant that it was wrong. To this day I can't come to terms with the fact that my father played a part in so much destruction. He was involved in a criminal business where many people were killed, more were put behind bars for decades and countless more became addicted to cocaine and then crack cocaine. So many families have been, and continue to be, devastated by the failed war on drugs.

I wondered if Dad saw it this way, but I never asked him. I still wasn't able to ask my father the hard questions. I now realize that not asking was just another way for me to avoid my own feelings of disappointment, shame and sadness. When my sister and I visited Dad, or when he and I talked on the phone, he seldom mentioned his days in the smuggling business. I believe that he wanted us to be proud of him, and he was an expert at avoidance too. He almost never talked about what prison life was like for him. It was as if he had two separate lives: when we were sitting with him in the visiting room, he didn't acknowledge the man he was behind those cement walls. He was our daddy. That was it.

I didn't want my dad to be a criminal, and I did hold him accountable for his crimes, yet I had a choice. I could turn my back on him, or I could try to forgive him, knowing that he was in prison for life for what he did. He had been judged. He was serving his time. I was his daughter, who he loved. I chose to be loyal to my incarcerated father.

16

Cards and Letters

In 1984, when Dad was sentenced to life without parole, I was 2,500 miles away, raising three kids. Jessica, our daughter, had been born in late February 1983, when I was twenty-nine. Thanks to Mom, who co-signed a loan, Salvador and I were able to buy the fixer-upper Victorian house that we had been renting on Pryce Street, near downtown Santa Cruz. I painted all the rooms and Salvador planted the most beautiful gardens all around the house.

Dad was sent to super-max USP Marion for the next four years. He then was transferred to USP Lewisburg, Pennsylvania, where he spent ten years.

During all that time I didn't see my dad. He was too far away, in a part of the country where I had never been, and I was busy with the day-to-day responsibilities of my family. Lyn was working full-time and only got away to see Dad once in USP Marion and maybe twice in USP Lewisburg.

Sol, Mom, Jessica and Chavo with me and Salvador, Easter 1985.

That didn't mean Dad and I lost touch. Quite the opposite. I was more connected to Dad than ever before. We wrote often, he called every now and then, and he sent birthday cards that his grandchildren adored, made by prison artists and featuring cartoon characters like Daffy Duck and Pluto.

During this time, Dad even managed to give us what turned out to be one of our family's greatest joys. Before he was arrested, he had paid a Canadian breeder for a Rottweiler puppy from a future litter. Now that he couldn't have a dog, he convinced me to let the breeder give the puppy to us. At first I was totally against it.

"Ber, the kids need a dog," he said during one of our phone conversations.

"Dad, I have enough on my plate without raising a puppy."

He persisted, and it turned out that everyone but me wanted the dog. Finally I caved in, and on a sunny Saturday morning we drove to the San Francisco airport to pick up our ten-week-old Rottweiler puppy. Salvador named her Mia.

Our whole family fell in love with that dog. Chavo and Sol played with her endlessly. For me, Mia took over where Pierre left off. I adored her, and particularly enjoyed letting her get up on the couch and climb—all 110 pounds of her—into my lap. Now that she was part of the family, I remembered from my own experience with Pierre how much a dog would enrich the lives of my children.

When Jessica was two, I enrolled in an internship program at the Santa Cruz Women's Health Center. I was soon hired part-time as a medical assistant for a gynecologist. Inspired by my mother's career path, I too chose a profession in health services.

After a year of learning as much as I could in the front and back offices, I saw an ad in the local paper for an accelerated program for professionals to get a bachelor's degree in health services administration. Applicants were required to have a two-year degree from a junior college, which I did have. The clincher was that I only had to attend classes one night a week in San Jose, an hour's drive from Santa Cruz. We didn't have the savings to pay for college, but that didn't deter me one bit. I took out student loans.

I was motivated to go to college in order to help my family. I wanted to succeed for Salvador and our kids, and for myself.

Past financial hardships only strengthened my determination. I set up a desk in one of the back rooms, got a computer and took on my aspirations with Mia lying at my feet and Salvador watching over the kids when I had a deadline to turn in a research paper.

In 1989, when I finished the program at the age of thirty-six, I had finally fulfilled my mother's dream to have one of her daughters graduate from college.

Degree in hand, I applied for a position at the Santa Cruz County Public Health Department. A month later I was hired as an HIV test counselor. My first assignment in public health was on the front lines fighting the AIDS epidemic. Within three years I was promoted to director of the HIV test program, with over twelve testing sites located throughout the county.

Based on my supervisor's advice, I decided to return to college in 1993 for my master's degree at San Jose State University. Supported by my department, I flexed my schedule and drove over mountainous Highway 17 to San Jose three times a week for two years until, in the spring of 1995, I graduated with a master's degree in public health.

That same year another dream came true. My precious mother moved permanently to Santa Cruz to be with me and her teenage grandkids. My mom retired from the Centers for Disease Control after an exalted career in which she had moved up to a federal government rank that paid the equivalent and had the same job responsibilities as a PhD.

Her success and dedication to public health served as a role model for me in my evolving career.

Over the next ten years I was repeatedly promoted, eventually advancing to the senior management position of Service Chief, Division Director of Health Benefits. I think, though, that my greatest legacy for the Santa Cruz County Health Services Agency was the annual potluck employee Halloween Show, which I founded and which continues to this day. I recruited secretaries, top management and everyone in between to dance and act in skits like "Rocky Horror Picture Show," "Ghost Busters" and "Thriller." It was the premier morale booster of the year, filling the auditorium with witches, ghosts and goblins. I, of course, was in every show.

Me (in the white skirt) as a zombie in "Thriller" at the Santa Cruz County Health Services Agency potluck Halloween Show.

In 1996, after Dad had been in prison for twelve years, he was granted a temporary transfer from Lewisburg to Atlanta to be close by for a family visit. The family was gathering to attend my sister's wedding to Eric, the man she met after her relationship with Herb ended.

It was a strange feeling, driving into the USP Atlanta parking lot with my whole family packed into the car, all of us staring up at the massive stone fortress surrounded by guard towers and barbed-wire fences. My heart raced. *Our dad lives here*, I thought despairingly. This was my first time visiting Dad in a penitentiary.

I fidgeted with the car keys, trying to get them into a plastic zip-lock bag before we got out of the car. My sister and our grandma, who had left Atlanta long ago to live near her sisters in Florida, parked beside us. Mostly in silence, we walked together toward the front of the building. I reached over and took my twelve-year-old daughter's hand in mine. She would be meeting her grandfather for the first time.

We waited in line to fill out forms and then waited some more. Forty-five minutes later, we went through the metal detector and were led by a guard, along with other visitors, through two huge metal gates. I flinched as they clanged shut behind us, flashing back to the first time I heard that noise when I was seven, the day my daddy took me across the street from his bonding company into that scary Atlanta city jail.

One of the guards pointed to where we were to sit on a row of hard vinyl chairs in the visiting room. I expect he didn't try to speak to us because we wouldn't have heard him above the deafening noise in the massive space. Clutching my plastic bag with my car keys and coins for the junk food machines, I sat and looked around, not saying a word. Small children sat on their fathers' knees, families huddled around bags of popcorn and sodas, talking and laughing. My own family sat on either side of me, staring around the room in silence, just like me.

A feeling that I recognized as excitement stirred in my gut. It had been almost thirteen years since I had last seen Dad in Medellín. And now, any minute, he was going to come through the door.

When he did, it felt like floodwaters of love bursting through a dam. All of us were laughing, hugging, crying. That day, it didn't matter that we were in a prison visiting room. The joyful spirit of our reunion took over, and between smiles and stories we were a unit cocooned together as if no one else was in the room.

Since we had never stopped writing and sending pictures to one another during those many years apart, I felt natural and easy being with Dad. At one point he reached over, took my hand and held it for a long time. I was finally in the caring presence of my father. He had a way of making me feel good about being his daughter, prison or no prison.

LYN'S WEDDING WAS an elegant and joyful affair, held in the Emory University museum. I was the matron of honor; my daughter, Jessica, was a bridesmaid; and because our father could not be present, Sol stood in for him to give Lyn away to her husband-to-be.

When my sister got married, I had been raising my family with Salvador for sixteen years. I loved Salvador throughout that time, and his steady, reliable presence provided me with the emotional stability I needed to venture out and reach for my educational and career goals. At the same time, those broadening experiences were changing me in ways that meant I had less in common with Salvador.

While my sister was now happily married, I struggled with the painful realization that I was no longer content in my marriage. I tried to deny that I was unhappy. I wasn't in love with Salvador the way I had been, but I was too afraid to say that to him or even to myself. I avoided admitting how I felt by spending many evenings at the gym instead of at home with my family. And I started drinking. A lot. I convinced myself that drinking was just a way to let loose, to have fun and to enjoy being social, even when, at times, I was drunk in front of my kids.

It didn't occur to me that history was repeating itself. I was modeling the same behavior that, when I was a child, had left me confused and unsure of what was going to happen to me. No one had asked me how I felt about my mom disappearing, my dad going to jail or my parents eventually divorcing. Just like them, I didn't tell Salvador or our children how I was feeling or ask them how they felt. I didn't know how.

When I decided to move out of our Pryce Street home into my own apartment, my drinking escalated. The kids wanted to stay at the family home, so I was alone most nights in my apartment, drink in hand, crying with guilt and shame for breaking up my family, for being so selfish. In 1997, Salvador and I formalized our divorce. I did the best I could, but even now I haven't completely resolved my regrets over how my behavior affected my children and Salvador.

In 1998 I met Damon when I showed up to do HIV testing at an alcohol and drug treatment center where he worked as an intake counselor. Damon was outgoing and kind-hearted, and he had a professional career in the community similar to mine.

After we had been together for a year or so, Damon became determined to marry me before he turned fifty. He had never been married. At Thanksgiving, when we were with his family in Ventura, California, he corralled his nephews Andrew, Daniel, Dillon and Kelly, and his niece Rejeana, all under the age of twelve, into the bedroom. He told them that when he got down on one knee and asked me to marry him, they should start chanting "Marry him, Jeri."

The kids paraded back into the living room, where I was talking to Damon's sister. Damon got down on one knee and took my hand, and the sweet singsong chanting began: "Marry him, Jeri, marry him."

It was impossible to resist those adorable children, so after a pause I said, "Maybe." But the truth was I had no intention of getting married again.

Damon's fiftieth birthday came and went. He stopped asking me to marry him. Another year passed. One day while I was in Atlanta, visiting my sister, I was missing my sweet Damon so much. I realized that life, after all, was about creating memories. That evening I called him up and asked, "Damon, will you marry me?"

Silence. I held my breath.

At last he replied. "Maybe." We both broke out laughing and set a wedding date.

We were a team; some called us a power couple. Over the years we directed community fundraising events for the Santa Cruz AIDS Project and rode our bikes six hundred miles from San Francisco to Los Angeles in the AIDS LifeCycle. Damon had ten years of sobriety when I met him, and he dedicated his career to supporting others who were also seeking sobriety.

He helped me understand that I was using alcohol to avoid my painful emotions. I became more aware of my unhealthy coping behavior and began noticing when and why I was drinking. Over time, I started drinking less.

And I helped Damon too. I was instrumental in his applying for and getting a job at the Santa Cruz County Health Services Agency. I encouraged his decision to start a drug and alcohol intervention business that eventually took him all over the country, helping families get their loved ones into treatment. He was dedicated to serving others, never giving up on people's ability to make positive choices that would support their having fulfilling lives. I was so proud of him.

Damon and me on our wedding day.

In 1998, not long after my relationship with Damon began, Dad was transferred to USP Leavenworth, Kansas, right in the middle of the country and in the middle of nowhere. During the seven years he was incarcerated there, Lyn would fly in from the east coast and I would fly in from the west coast to visit him. We also continued our relationship with Dad through frequent phone calls and letters.

Then, when our father had been in prison for almost twenty years, along came the year 2000.

PART III

2000–2018

17

Blow My Hair Back

As the world charged into the new millennium, I changed too, in ways that both excited and frightened me. I was in a new relationship, yes. But much more than my love life was changing. Without much fanfare, the thick protective shield of the respectable, narrowly defined life that I had been building for decades cracked. I compare the feeling to what it was like giving birth. That baby was coming out no matter what. The new me wanted to be born, and all efforts I might make to prevent it were futile. I just could not resist the urge to break free of my ordinary, predictable life and dream bigger.

I wanted to be an entrepreneur and travel the world.

For twenty years I had been raising a family, getting college degrees and working a steady government job in the small town of Santa Cruz. I had many challenging and fulfilling experiences during this period, but now I was in my late forties with grown kids. The timing felt right for a bold move that could open me to new personal and professional heights. I wasn't exactly sure what I was going to do to manifest my dreams, but I decided to focus all my energy on making it happen.

On one especially miserable can-I-should-I-it-won't-work-you're-insane-to-leave-a-six-figure-job-to-jump-off-into-the-unknown day, I came home from work, plopped down on the couch with the life force gone out of me, and begged for one of those "you can do it, girl" signs to show up.

The phone rang. I walked across the room and answered it.

"This call is from a federal prison. This is a prepaid call. You will not be charged for this call. To accept this call, dial five now. To block future prepaid calls from this person, dial seven seven."

I pressed five and heard the voice of my father. "Ber!"

I took a deep breath and jumped at the chance to share my thoughts. "Dad, I want to start my own business. What do you think?"

He didn't hesitate for a second. "Jeri! You can do it. Think about working with Lyn and developing health care products for her company."

By this time my sister had been in her own successful skin care business for eleven years. Instead of taking the traditional route, as I had done, and obtaining a college degree, she had trained to become a master esthetician. She established a school of advanced medical skin care training, developed her own branded product line and opened the first medical spa in

Atlanta, in the prestigious Buckhead area. Her ambitious business endeavors inspired me.

By the end of my fifteen-minute conversation with Dad, I felt lighter. Was it a coincidence that Dad called and encouraged me to follow my dreams moments after I asked for a hopeful sign? Or was it an omen?

A FEW MONTHS LATER, another event occurred that fueled my evolving entrepreneurial spirit with a profound new purpose. Damon and I packed up the car and drove three hours from Santa Cruz to charming Calistoga, California, for a weekend in Napa Valley. After we had settled into our vacation suite for the evening, I poured myself a glass of wine, got out my knitting and flipped on the TV.

That night I watched the movie *The Shawshank Redemption* for the first time.

In *The Shawshank Redemption*, Andy Dufresne (played by Tim Robbins) is serving a life sentence in Shawshank State Penitentiary for murdering his wife, though he claims to be innocent. He befriends a fellow inmate, Red, played by Morgan Freeman. After nineteen years in prison, Andy escapes through a tunnel that he has dug from his cell wall into the sewer system below. Before leaving, he tells Red that if he is ever paroled, he should go to a particular field in Texas, where he will find a note and money.

Red does get paroled and finds the cache containing money and a letter asking him to come to Zihuatanejo, Mexico. Sparked by the hope that Andy will be waiting for him, Red violates his parole and crosses the border. I was transfixed. When I saw the men reunite on a sandy white beach in Mexico, I was overcome with hope.

Could I be Dad's Andy, his hopeful passage to a life of freedom earned investing his heart and soul in a legitimate family business? What if Dad and I worked together? Could I help him change his karma? He couldn't undo the harm he had done to people through his drug smuggling, but maybe he could do good for others. Maybe, by supporting my aspirations, he too could be responsible for healthy, positive outcomes for other people.

I returned to Santa Cruz and awaited Dad's next call.

"Ber!"

After greeting each other and sharing news back and forth, I was ready to pop the question.

"Hey, Dad. I've been thinking. I would like to hire you to be the director of research and development for my new company, LJR Inc. [Lyn and Jeri Ross Incorporated]."

"Really?" he said with childlike exuberance. "Well, I think that would be just great."

THE CHALLENGE WAS ON! In less than a week, and after several more conversations, Dad and I decided to develop a more efficient and convenient way for women to take their vitamins by applying a lotion that would infuse micronutrients through the skin, to be transported throughout the body via the bloodstream. Days later, our father, as the company's R & D director, sent me the following handwritten official summation:

> The basic premise for this invention is to enhance penetration of sufficient orthomolecular concentrations of micronutrients in blood serum levels to induce cellular biochemical activity resulting in optimal health of the human body.

I was astounded that Dad could craft this kind of technical description. I couldn't wait to see what he was going to do next!

Dad took his assignment very seriously. He found article after article in the newspapers and magazines he read daily about vitamins, business models, funding resources, retail trends and marketing ideas, and he neatly clipped each one, highlighted the relevant portions and sent them to me for review. He gave me lists of things to look up on the Internet, print out and send to him to study, including technical patents. Before long I had files, binders and boxes filled with research materials. He had no access to a computer, and the inmate version of "cut and paste" was exactly that: typed words cut, with scissors, from one section and glued to another. It took hours.

As fledgling scientists pursuing our dream, we spoke as often as we could. Dad called me over and over, patching together those fifteen-minute calls so he had enough time to convey his concepts and formulation ideas. His energy was boundless and so powerful that one day I told him his excitement for our project was blowing my hair back as if I were riding a motorcycle.

From then on, whenever he had a breakthrough finding he would say to me, "Oh! Oh! You're never going to believe what I uncovered! Put your helmet on! I'm going to blow your hair back!"

My hand quivered as I held the phone receiver to my ear and listened, feeling the knot in my stomach pulse along with each ring. While I was intrigued and stimulated by my new scientific course of study, I was terrified of calling scientists, chemists or physicians to dig for answers that would help with our invention. Dad never let me avoid those calls, no matter how much I resisted.

"Jeri, get in touch with Dr. Braidon in Ireland. He heads up the research lab that is studying transdermal delivery of pharmaceuticals. Find out what will get through the skin and what excipients he recommends."

"Dad, he won't talk to me," I said.

"Yes, he will."

"Why would he talk to me?"

"Because you'll call him and tell him that you work in public health and you are interested in creating a transdermal vitamin product."

"But, Dad, he's a scientist. I'm not."

"Honey, you're doing such a good job from scratch to where you are now. You're my champ. Get out in the ring and keep fighting. I know that you'll be a winner because you're not going to let anyone or anything defeat you. Everywhere you turn, you see that you're on the right path. I want this for you, and that's what motivates me to put everything I've got into the project. I'm the proudest dad in the whole world of my look-alike daughter. My heart hurts with how much I love you, Sweetie."

I jumped when a man answered. "Hello, this is Dr. Braidon," he said in an Irish accent that I could barely understand.

"Hello, Dr. Braidon. I'm calling from California in the United States. Thank you for taking my call. I'm Jeri Ross, CEO of a clinical skin care company, and we are developing a transdermal product for taking vitamins through the skin. I would be so pleased if you could answer a few questions."

"Why, yes, of course," he replied. "How can I help you?"

I had my prepared questions written and ready. I took a breath. "Can you tell me the most effective processing preparation for a vitamin to penetrate the skin? Micronized, chelated or esterified?"

"Ms. Ross, my department does not work with vitamins, only pharmaceutical drugs. I really don't know who would be best to refer you to," he said, and added, "You must be cautious with your project. Any product manufactured and marketed that claims biological reactions in the body would have to be approved by the FDA."

"I understand," I replied, feeling defeat punch me in the stomach. FDA approval took years and tons of money. I hung up and stared into the glare of my computer screen.

When Dad called, I gave him the bad news.

With no hesitation, he responded, "What we're trying to do is not easy. It's a good thing that you're a problem solver."

And sure enough, I did figure out how to avoid the problem: we just didn't make any claims that would require FDA approval.

A few days later I received this letter from Dad.

> *You hired your dad to work on the formulas for you not because he was a scientist, but because he was not in a "box." You're now at the experimental stage in your own development as an entrepreneur. Have FAITH in what you have and what you know nobody else knows.*
>
> *Every morning in Africa, a gazelle wakes up.*
>
> *It knows that it must run faster than the fastest lion or it will be killed.*
>
> *Every morning a lion wakes up.*
>
> *It knows that it must outrun the slowest gazelle or it will starve to death.*
>
> *It doesn't matter whether you are a lion or a gazelle.*
>
> *When the sun rises, you better be running.*

Just when my doubts clouded my faith in "what I had and what I knew nobody else knew," there was Dad, not letting me cave in, not allowing me to be a quitter. I had to wake up every day at sunrise and start running again until I accomplished my dream. Dad was going to make sure of that.

A YEAR OR SO into our endeavor, Dad called. The moment I pressed five to accept the call, he burst out with "Ber! I think I've blown a fuse! You know the eighty-two-year-old man's patent you sent me to study? I found a secret here for our formula! Listen to this!"

With the elation of a child running through an amusement park, he began reading the patent abstract.

> A composition having therapeutic and cosmetic effects is comprised of an effective concentration of methyl nicotinate (niacin) in dilutants. When such a composition is topically applied, the methyl nicotinate acts to increase circulation in the area of application. The methyl nicotinate also acts as a facilitator to promote the transdermal penetration of the vitamins, minerals, and other nutrients into the skin.

He ended with a slight pause and a big "Wow!" I laughed with delight.

"Okay, Dad. I'll see if I can order this ingredient, methyl nicotinate, and use it on myself to see what happens."

As it turned out, methyl nicotinate was the "secret sauce" that made our product unique and effective, unlike anything else on the market.

AT THIS POINT in my life, I was working full-time in my public health job and working with Dad on our LJR project.

When Damon suggested we take a vacation, I agreed, but after we had driven three hours to Avila Beach, I felt unsettled and guilty about taking time off from my work with Dad. Whenever I had a spare minute, I believed I should be working.

The next day, while riding a mountain bike through spectacular forests and along the brilliant Pacific coast, I had a small epiphany. I was never "off" the project because I was always learning about myself, life and my relationship with my father. This, not the development of a skin care product, was the real project. What we were doing together wasn't about the product: it was about us discovering and growing our very special father-daughter connection.

I realized that my dad was coaching me, on the outside, to be what he had to be inside jail: unbreakable. My sister and I had begun to receive letters from men who knew our father, who had lived with him for years on the inside at Leavenworth. These men praised him for being a mentor who led by example, a man who showed them how to change their lives for the better by being strong mentally and physically. According to the letters, Dad was revered for his ability to work out harder than almost any other man there, even those much younger than him. He was highly respected, and knowing that brought me closer to him. My dad had to survive years in prison with no possibility of parole, but in no way was incarceration going to crush his warrior spirit. The project was giving me an opportunity to learn more about my dad's resilience.

Throughout that time, Dad sent me philosophical, technical and inspirational letters. I read these letters over and over again, spellbound. I felt as if I was seeing this man for the first time. As well, I had the comforting feeling that he was now being the parent he wasn't able to be for most of my life.

Together, Dad and I learned about the magic and mystery of cellular biology. Dad wrote about cells as if they had their own personalities. He told me that the better we could understand the cell, the more effectively we could develop our product, because we would know what the little cells needed and wanted.

A letter Dad sent just before Damon and I went on our holiday delighted me with its quirky inventiveness.

> *The little cell knows what it wants to let in and work with because GOD (good ole dirt) created it. What that little cell knows from millions of years of life is that it lives on nutrients from the plants that grow from dirt, and that any chemical from plants is cell-friendly. The SECRET of why the fat-soluble ingredients will go into the skin is that the cells communicate with each other. That little cell is extremely complex and smart. It is not a non-knowing living unit. Each cell can be thought of as having a life of its own.*

The letter ended: "My beautiful cellular number two daughter. These revelations are not for me, they are for you. I am simply the carrier molecule." Each time I read it, I laughed at Dad's description of himself as the carrier molecule. My laughter was opening me to him.

In July 2001 I confirmed my travel arrangements to visit Dad at USP Leavenworth for our first face-to-face business meeting. He officially termed our two-day meeting the Trans-Dermal Delivery (TDD) Summit. Through the years I had coped with the fact that my father was in prison by trying to put that reality out of my mind. I didn't picture Dad working on our project in the confines of a prison cell. But now I was preparing to visit him. The mental image of me walking away from him on our last day, leaving him behind bars, tormented me, especially now that I felt so much closer to him. Just thinking about that moment brought tears to my eyes.

In early August I boarded a plane to attend the TDD Summit at Leavenworth maximum-security federal penitentiary. My suitcase was full of books about micronutrients and scientific journals, along with my silky, my calming piece of fabric, tucked into a side pocket. The four-hour flight took me to Kansas City, where I rented a car.

"Is this trip business or pleasure?" the man behind the Alamo counter asked.

His question made me pause. My first thought was, Well, I guess you couldn't call going to a maximum-security penitentiary "pleasure," but I *was* on a family visit. It was a business trip as well, because Dad was the director of R & D for LJR.

"It's sort of both," I said.

He gave me the keys to my new ride, a silver Toyota Corolla, and I drove out of the parking lot and fifty miles to the Holiday Inn Express near the prison.

I awoke at six the next morning to get an early start on the long process of visiting an inmate in prison. At 8 a.m.

I entered the parking lot of Leavenworth penitentiary and drove up to a built-in speaker located at the base of a cement tower.

A stern male voice boomed at me, "What is the purpose of your visit?"

"I'm here to visit my father, inmate Harold Rosenthal," I responded.

"You may pass and park over to the left side of the parking lot."

"Okay, thank you," I said before driving exactly as he had directed me.

As always, I left my purse and all other possessions in the trunk. I walked in the still morning air toward the massive gray stone building with bars and barbed wire. My stomach churned. It wasn't my first time visiting Dad in prison, but it never got easier. Once inside, I entered the check-in area, filled out the paperwork and sat down to wait my turn, with my plastic zip-lock bag in my lap.

When my name was called, I went through the metal detector, held out my hand to be stamped and was led by a guard, along with other visitors, through three huge metal gates that clanged shut behind us. I was assigned table number five, moved where the guard pointed, and sat down. Within minutes another guard came up to me and said firmly, "Ma'am, you're sitting on the inmate's side. You need to change to the other side." I did as I was told.

I shifted from side to side in the hard chair, unable to get comfortable, especially when I thought about how my father had to live his life within these strict confines when his true nature made him better suited for the wilds of the jungle. Yes, he was in prison because he broke the law, but in that moment I couldn't shake a deep sadness. It seemed wrong to me that in order for us to be together, he had to be temporarily released from his cage and escorted to the visiting room by guards.

Dad didn't look sad when he appeared, though. In fact, he was practically skipping with joy. He was wearing a clean, neatly ironed brown shirt and pants and looked just as well-groomed as always. In fact, he looked great! The skin on his face was soft, and he had color in his cheeks. I rushed into his arms. We held each other, crying.

We sat down, wiped away our tears and settled into becoming reacquainted after the two years since my last visit. I could stay with Dad for six uninterrupted hours, which allowed us to dive deep into our TDD Summit agenda, so much better than the fifteen-minute phone calls. However, pens and paper were not allowed in the visiting room, so everything we talked about had to be drawn from, and noted to, memory.

I began by telling Dad that I had started off plagued with doubts, but that as we uncovered more and more clues to creating our invention, I began to realize that we could really be onto something. I explained to him that I was feeling more confident about myself. I also wanted him to know how much his coaching was helping me.

"Dad," I said, "I'm beginning to understand that you are encouraging me not only to think outside the box, but to live outside the box. You certainly have done that!" We both laughed at the irony of that remark.

For hours we talked about surfactants, fatty acid esters, patents, cellular metabolism, tocopherols, glutathione, niacin, lipoic acid, natural progesterone and, of course, transdermal delivery systems. Conversing with Dad about these topics was like finding a lemonade stand in the desert. We recognized that we both had a passion for learning about human biology, especially the life of cells.

I smiled when Dad told me, "We think alike. Did you know that?"

"Dad, didn't you tell me earlier today to read Dr. Lester Packer's book *The Antioxidant Miracle*? I was reading that book on the plane out here!"

The next day, Dad told me over and over again how much he wanted his two-both, his girls, to be together. He also told me that I was doing a really good job with the project and that it would come together.

"Ber, your daddy loves you so much. I'm doing this for you."

The hours passed like minutes until, at two thirty on the dot, the guard yelled, "Time's up. Visiting hours are over."

We hugged one final time, our eyes shiny with tears. Dad lined up against the wall with the other inmates, and I got in line with the visitors. Here I was at that dreaded moment. I looked around the visiting room and saw a little girl, about four years old, reaching out and crying for her dad as he moved away from her to line up. I felt exactly like that little girl, unable to understand why my dad couldn't just walk out with me.

On the plane back to Santa Cruz, I opened my wallet and found the little yellow sticky notes that Dad had sneaked into the visiting area. As I read what he wrote—"So glad you came, miss you so much"—I wept. I stared out the window at the endless sky and then to the earth below. The vastness seemed like a big crevasse between us. Physically I was moving farther and farther away from my father, but thanks to our project I was also moving closer and closer to him.

The next morning the phone rang. I expected it to be Dad, wanting to know that I was home safe.

"Hello!" I said in my best cheery voice.

"Jeri." It was my sister.

"Hey, Lyn! It went great!" I exclaimed. "Dad looked so good. He has transformed himself into a scientist."

I told her that Dad wanted us to be closer as sisters and best friends, and that I did too.

"Jeri," she said, "I know you and Dad have been studying vitamins to formulate a body product, but I was thinking the other day that I could really use a good cellulite product. Maybe you and Dad could apply what you're finding out about vitamins and transdermal delivery to that kind of a product."

I paused for a moment, thinking about her proposition. The commercial potential of a cellulite product was exciting, especially with my sister's already existing wholesale accounts.

"Okay, Lyn. I like the idea. I'll talk it over with Dad."

When Dad called later that day, I said, "Lyn wants us to create a cellulite product. What do you think?"

"Well, she's the big boss. If she wants a cellulite product, we should do that. What do you think?".

"I already went online to find out more about the ingredients in cellulite products. We can create a product similar to what's out there, get some sales going and keep working on our TDD vitamin product as planned."

He hesitated for a moment. "Jeri, we can't do that."

"What do you mean?" I asked.

"We must go with our creative vision and not with what others are doing. You have to come up with new and different products. This product has to work for your success in your new business."

WITHIN A FEW DAYS I received this message in a letter from Dad:

> *A creative researcher ... scientist or chemist thinks outside what is the norm and CREATES something new. Now it will be your own projects you work on. It will keep you up at night sometimes or wake you up during the night with thoughts you write down. Linus Pauling said he does it. And so will you. A creative person is one who envisions something, puts it together, takes little advice from others and sees it through to fruition. He does not let others influence his vision, right or wrong, he plugs ahead. That's you. She does not know it cannot be done.*

I read Dad's letter over several times. A soft feeling came over me, like when a calm rain replenishes a garden with the elements needed for life to exist, for flowers to bloom. I sank into a state of reverie, as if the project was raining on me, encouraging me to trust.

As I let the sensation sink in, I realized that Dad and I could apply our transdermal micronutrient discoveries to a cellulite formula. We could create a skin lotion that would be infused with vitamin ingredients to help women prevent and reduce their cellulite. I was beginning to see the potential, and the connection to our original product idea.

MORE MONTHS OF research went by, and many hours of studying the biology of cellulite. After trying a multitude of cellulite products, Dad and I selected a company to manufacture our products. It was a world-renowned firm that specialized in advanced skin penetration or transdermal delivery technology.

"This is it," I said to myself as I drove into the parking lot of the company's laboratory in Pittsburg, California.

I pulled down the sun visor to check myself in the mirror. My hands shook a little as I made minor adjustments to my makeup and hair, final preparations for the performance of a lifetime. I studied my face for a long moment. I looked nervous. In my head I heard the people I was about to meet say, "We are the expert scientists. You are not. Sorry we can't help you." I pictured myself having to tell Dad that in spite of all our work, we had failed.

I would have to tell him that putting my helmet on wasn't going to help.

I picked up my folder marked "Cellulite Formula," opened the car door and walked into the building.

"Hello. I have an appointment. My name is Jeri Ross," I said, and named Lyn's company.

"Hi, Jeri," the receptionist said with a bright smile. "You can wait in our conference room. The door on your left."

"Thanks," I responded with my own bright, fake-it-till-you-make-it smile. Within minutes I was shaking hands with a rep and the lab director.

After giving me a brief overview of the company's services and technology, Fred asked, "How can we help you, Jeri? I understand that yours is a clinical skin care company and you want to formulate a cellulite product for your customers. Is that correct?"

"Yes," I replied in my most professional voice. "Our R & D department has been working on a formula that we feel would have better results using your transdermal technology." I left out the part about our R & D department being located at Leavenworth penitentiary. "I brought our preliminary formula and would like to discuss it with you. I prepared these letters of nondisclosure for you to sign."

I passed the documents to both men. After they signed, I pulled out the formula and held my breath. The information written on this piece of paper could change my life. The room was silent as they read. I hoped they couldn't hear my heart thumping in my chest.

The lab director paused, looked up at me and said, "I have never seen these kinds of ingredients in a cellulite product before. Why do you have natural progesterone in your formula?"

Just as Dad had trained me, I responded as the creative inventor who does what has never been done before. "From my research, I found out that one of the key reasons women have cellulite is estrogen dominance promoting fat storage in the lower layers of the skin. My proposed product formula would infuse the skin with natural progesterone to curtail estrogen production at the cellular level. That is why I am interested in your transdermal delivery system. I need these active ingredients to penetrate in order to obtain good results."

The rep spoke next. "Jeri, my first response is that this product will be expensive to manufacture. You have quite a list of ingredients here. Did you know that we already manufacture a cellulite cream?"

"I didn't know that," I replied. "What ingredients does it have in it?"

"The main ingredient is caffeine," he said.

"What else?" I asked.

"That's it. Just caffeine. You could easily private-label the product we're already producing for much less cost."

"Does it work?" I asked.

"We sell a lot of it," he replied.

"I have to make a product that works or I can't represent it," I said. "In theory, I know that my formula will work. I'd like you to make a prototype that we can use in clinical studies." My voice grew stronger as I flexed my small but growing courage muscle. "Can you do that?" I asked.

The room went silent again. Every part of me willed their response, Yes! Yes! Do it!

Looking down at the formula and then back at me, the lab director said, "We can do that. It will take a couple of months. We'll have to get you a cost. Also keep in mind that when you are ready to manufacture your product, our minimum quantity is five thousand units."

"That's fine," I heard myself saying, even though I had no idea how much five thousand units would cost or how we could sell that much product. I shook their hands, walked out the door and got in my car. Before I turned the key, I let out a loud "Yahooooo!"

Five months later I got a call from the research group that had conducted an eight-week study with the prototype.

"Jeri, we're getting results. The participants want to know how soon they can get more of your cellulite product."

I shouted inside my head, "We did it, Dad," as I burst into excited laughter.

I was so eager to tell him the news! I waited for him to call, then waited some more. Two days went by. Four days. Six. Finally, a week later, I got a letter from Dad. He was in lock-down again.

When I didn't get my regular phone calls, it could mean that something terrible had happened to him, or it could be that he was in lockdown, only allowed to leave his cell to take a shower. It was against prison policy to give information on the status of an inmate to family members, so even when we did call to ask about our dad, we never learned anything that let us know if he was okay.

I would have to send him the news in a letter. He might not be able to use the phone for weeks. I reread his sweet letter:

> *I worship my angels. I am thinking about my two beautiful daughters and how BLESSED I am to have such great daughters that I love so much and love me. That's what I always wanted. I so much enjoy doing things with you girls. The fellas want to know why I'm not into watching sports. They all do. Cause it's not as exciting as CELLULITE. I just want my two-both to be together. That is what I want for you. And it is coming true. Love you so much, Ber, Your Daddy*

As always, he didn't complain or say anything that would cause me to worry about him. I marveled at his ability to be positive despite being locked down twenty-three hours a day for days on end.

We spent the next few months negotiating pricing with the manufacturer and creating package designs. Lyn was in a state of disbelief that Dad and I had managed to develop an effective cellulite formula and had contracted with a lab to manufacture the product. She was busy managing her spa and wholesale company and had left everything to the two of us so far. She also told me that she had been a little afraid that working together might hurt rather than help our relationship. But now that we had proven we could do the job, she got over her nervousness and started to join in the excitement of the project, which made Dad ecstatic.

Oct 2003
Hi Sweetheart,

It's Sunday afternoon and I'm thinking about you, which I do a lot during the day and nite too. I am really anxious for your product to get going and making money so you can be working full time on DERMED products with Lyn. So far it sounds like you are getting back good responses and that is encouraging. WOW!! Sure is all coming together and I am loving every minute of it. Lyn is really looking forward to you working with her too so you can do more things together. She loves you so much. You both look so good and to think you're both mine and I love you both lots and lots.

Love my Ber mucho … Dad

Dad and I had accomplished a significant breakthrough. And having my sister on board certainly gave me more confidence.

My first trip back to our business headquarters in Atlanta confirmed my destiny as an evolving entrepreneur.

My sister had arranged for me to conduct sales training, create spa service protocols and pose for promotional shots. She also took me to Manhattan to meet her PR firm director, who was slated to help us launch this newest addition to the product family. I hadn't been in New York City since I was in grade school.

After we settled into our room at the W Hotel in Times Square, we paraded around the city while I gawked up at the skyscrapers. The next morning at eight, we met in our hotel lobby to be briefed about the appointments made on our behalf with beauty editors of major magazines. Our marathon schedule was fittingly called "desk side trots." For two full days we rode around the city, climbing in and out of yellow cabs and elevators, being whisked up to the top floors of the same skyscrapers I'd been gawking at. We pitched our product to *Vogue, Marie Claire, O Magazine, Shape, Self* and so many more. I was in a trance-like state of wonder. Was I really in New York City talking to major magazines about a product that Dad and I had created? It felt surreal.

On our last day in the city, we took a cab to Madison Avenue to meet with the president of an international marketing and distribution company. After the meeting, the company agreed to represent our line of cellulite products.

I signed the deal, and two months later I was on a plane to the corporate headquarters of Victoria's Secret in Columbus, Ohio, to pitch my brand to one of the premier women's retailers in the world. As I stared down at the brown-and-green patchwork landmass passing rapidly beneath the jet, I felt like a character in a movie. Was I really me?

My dim yet recognizable reflection in the plane's porthole window looked back at me and silently said, There is that woman who was afraid to call scientists, to take a risk, who doubted her own ability and credibility. That woman, YOU, is now meeting up with big-time, multimillion-dollar retailers to tell them about her products, her formulation, her creation.

I reflected on Dad's words: *Never lose sight of the vision. You can do it. I believe in you.*

Two weeks after my trip, I was in my home office when the phone rang. Moments later, I hung up the phone in shock. Our cellulite products would be featured in the January issue of the Victoria's Secret catalog! Between squeals of delight, I jumped around my living room, fell to the floor, rolled over on my back and shook my legs in the air with uncontrollable relief and pure, uninhibited joy.

THE TIME HAD COME. In 2006, after months of using all my vacation days to travel around the country promoting my products, I took early retirement from the Santa Cruz County Health Services Agency, at age fifty-two. Even though I was proud of my success, I felt conflicted about my new identity as a person selling a cellulite product when for years I had been dedicated to saving lives in public health.

This dilemma eventually helped me see how I could incorporate my health background into product-marketing approaches that emphasized self-care. I developed a three-pronged approach to cellulite reduction that included

Lyn and me (left) working together in her medical spa in Atlanta.

exercise and nutritional wellness along with topical cellulite products. As a credentialed health educator, I wrote magazine articles that promoted the idea of women having a positive relationship with their bodies. I wasn't saving lives, but I felt better knowing that I could continue to promote health, especially women's health.

With the help of my New York marketing reps, we expanded into global markets. I traveled to product launches in Sweden, France, Belgium, Italy, Mexico, Australia, Taiwan and Singapore.

Like many people, including my mom, Damon was concerned at first about me giving up my day job, but now he was right behind Dad as my second-biggest fan. He was my constant companion and sounding board, helping me with all aspects of the business, from filling orders in the warehouse to attending product pitches in Hong Kong. And while every day unfolded without my knowing exactly where business prospects would take me, my husband was my rock. He embraced the uncertainty, as I did, with trust and promise. We were having the time of our lives.

In March 2007, my sister and I decided to go to Cosmoprof, the world's largest beauty trade show, in Bologna, Italy. I had just started reading *Eat, Pray, Love* by Elizabeth Gilbert. I tossed the book in my purse with the intention, like Elizabeth, of letting my travels open me to new spiritual insights.

On the train from Milano to Bologna, Lyn and I sat next to each other, wearing identical black velvet Cossack caps that she had bought for our trip. After a while she reached into her bag and said, "When one of my girlfriends found out I was going to Italy, she said I should get this book." She pulled out *Eat, Pray, Love.*

I hollered with delight, "I'm reading that same book!"

For the next hour we sat elbow to elbow, two-both, gliding through the Italian countryside, turning the pages of a new and exciting chapter in our lives.

18

Aging

Dad had been transferred from Leavenworth to USP Coleman, another maximum-security federal facility located about fifty miles north of Orlando, Florida. While he was closer to Lyn, the prison was still four hundred miles and a six-hour drive from Atlanta. By now Dad was in his mid-seventies. He did the best he could to take care of his health by working out, not smoking, and buying vitamins and vegetables in the commissary. Nevertheless, at his age the move was hard on him. Much worse were the constant lockdowns imposed on all inmates when there was an incident, like a stabbing or a fight, between two or a few men. During lockdowns, all phone calls and family visits are prohibited, and all inmates are locked in their cells twenty-three hours per day, with only one hour to shower and walk in the yard.

October 28, 2007

Hi Sweetheart

It's going to be months of lockdowns and it gets worse by the day.

February 2008

Hi Sweetheart

Well, you guessed it. We're locked down again. Maybe out in another week. I am so sorry you have to go through this. But it is only a bump in the road. We have so much to be thankful for.

July 2008

Hi Sweetheart,

Still don't know when we'll get out. I know you both are going West. Will talk with you when I get out. Give my love to all the family out there, my grandchildren and grand-dog. [He was referring to Damon's and my adored dog, given to us by my son Sol.] This prison stuff is a bummer.

December 2008

My little sweetheart Girl,

I was so disappointed I couldn't call you. I know you have so much great news. Looks like we'll be locked down until mid-January. I wanted to see my baby so bad.

In March 2010 they found Dad passed out on the floor of his cell during a lockdown. He was seventy-eight years old. They rushed him to Leesburg Medical Center, where they performed an emergency triple bypass that saved his life. For the next several months he was weak and disoriented, trying to recover from major heart surgery in prison.

Just as he was getting back to his normal self, he was rushed to the hospital again, this time for gastrointestinal bleeding from a duodenal ulcer. He was given eight units of blood and, miraculously, survived. A few days later he was deemed stable enough to return to the prison, only to be rushed to the hospital a third time in extreme pain. Laboratory testing determined that he had contracted septicemia—a life-threatening bacterial blood infection—from the blood transfusions.

During this time, Lyn and I were receiving little information about what was happening with our father. The only messages were from inmates who knew Dad and who had asked their own family members to contact us. We called and wrote the warden and finally were told that the only time the prison releases information about an inmate's health is when the inmate is dying or dead. The only good thing about that response was it suggested Dad must not be dying or they would have notified us. At least, that was what we hoped it meant.

On March 19, 2011, we finally received this letter from him:

> *My 2 beautiful Daughters,*
>
> *Honeys I'm so sorry for all of this sickness and I'm feeling bad. They keep me chained up to a bed by my feet and one arm. My body is in pain and deteriorating. They let me walk in the hall for ten or fifteen minutes, but that's not enough. My legs are swollen and hurt. My skin is all broken open. My caseworker came to see me and said she would try to get me into a prison medical hospital so they don't have to keep me in chains. I'm a daddy with a broken heart. Keep your spir-spirs up for me. I love you girls, my only loves.*

Dad wasn't taken to a prison hospital. But he once again recovered enough to be transported back to his cell at USP Coleman. It was around this time that both Lyn and I encouraged him to request a transfer to Federal Correctional Complex (FCC) Butner in North Carolina, a facility that specialized in geriatric care for federal inmates. His response was "I don't need to get transferred. I need to get out."

Two months later, Coleman's Warden Middlebrooks told Dad that he was retiring. While Dad never told us much about his life inside, from the little he did say, and from the letters my sister and I got every once in a while from the men who were incarcerated with him, we got the sense that Dad was like the mayor in every prison where he was held. He gained the trust and respect not only of the inmates but also of the administration, guards, medical staff, caseworkers and wardens. In one of his progress reports from 2004, I read "Mr. Rosenthal has an excellent rapport with staff."

Warden Middlebrooks asked my father if there was anything he could do for him before he left. Instead of requesting a transfer to FCC Butner, which would have been far more comfortable, with fewer restrictions and with access to excellent medical care, Dad told the warden he wanted to be transferred to Atlanta to be closer to his daughter Lyn.

That relocation was extremely difficult for Dad since he was still weak and in recovery from his triple bypass and the bout with septicemia. The good part was there were fewer lockdowns. The bad part was he had to learn the inner workings of a different prison, and he had to start from scratch, building trusting relationships again. As mentally and physically tough as our dad was, he had now been incarcerated for twenty-six years, and he was old. How would he, at eighty, stay safe in a new violent and aggressive environment? Lyn and I kept trying to convince him to transfer to Butner, but he told us that he wouldn't get as many visits there, so that was out.

"I'll make it work here," he said.

His obstinacy frustrated me no end. Lyn told me how almost every time she talked with him he complained about the food and the small cell. The environment was loud, with inmates shouting all day and into the night. What bothered him most, though, was that he now had to share his cell. Lyn and I could tell how much he was enduring, and it pained us to know how uncomfortable he was.

19

Hawk

In 2010, when Dad started having major health issues, I was in my eighth year as CEO of LJR Inc. I had faced my fears, transformed myself into an entrepreneur and realized my dreams to travel the world. Yet I was feeling more and more unsettled. I sensed that I was at another crossroads, but I couldn't figure out why I was so restless. I suspected that it had something to do with my relationship with my father. In working with Dad, I had started to allow those bars around my heart to melt, healing a part of me that had been closed off for years. Something was changing, but at the time all I knew was that I was in turmoil. I had no idea what to do about it.

In August 2010 I traveled to Atlanta to be with my sister on her birthday. One evening, long after the sun had set, we were sitting together in her sunroom, drinking red wine. I was going on and on about how out of sync I felt with myself.

Lyn picked up her phone, wrote something on a sticky note and handed it to me.

"Chloé's a wonderful life coach," she told me. "Why don't you give her a call?"

I called Chloé the next day. Working with Chloé Taylor Brown, I finally recognized that for most of my life I had looked for the approval of others in order to feel safe. I didn't speak up for myself and did my best to please others thinking that if I didn't I wouldn't be loved.

Through coaching I learned that my soul self, or what Chloé called my *isness,* would help me awaken to the unique expression of my higher nature, and this awakening would help me learn that I didn't need anyone outside me to make me right with the world. I would realize that the most important person who needed to love me was me.

Knowing this was helpful, but, honestly, I was thrown into a state of confusion. Oh, shit! I thought. Now what? How was I going to figure out the real me when I had been living for decades as the afraid, conditioned and what-I-thought-was-safe me?

ONE NIGHT IN late December, I lay in bed, thinking about the work I had done with Chloé. What would happen, I wondered, if I dedicated 2011 to an adventure to learn more about my *isness*? Could I follow my heart and trust that it would lead me to answers? I wasn't sure how to embark on a journey listening to the whispers of my soul, but I was willing to give it a try.

I didn't have to wait long.

Two weeks after New Year's Day, my soul spoke up. I was in line at Staff of Life, a natural foods store, flipping through the pages of *Spirituality and Health,* when I came across a tiny image of a white-haired woman in a cowgirl hat holding the reins of a majestic black horse. I read the small ad: "Gathering the Soul in the Wilderness: Women's Retreat at the Blacktail Ranch in Wolf Creek, Montana."

The checkout line shifted forward. Should I put the magazine back or should I buy it? I reached over to return it to the shelf, but found myself tossing it into my basket instead.

Within thirty minutes I was at my computer, typing in the web address for the retreat. A page popped up. The retreat would be led by psychotherapist Connie Myslik-McFadden, who had spent years living in Montana, riding horses. As I read, I went still inside. "Everyone has aspects of their being that are unknown, untamed, wild. You are invited to explore your inner and outer wilderness in beautiful Montana. Experience the healing power of mountains, forests, rivers, sunshine, big sky, and the companionship of kindred spirits." A tingle rippled up my spine.

I scrolled down. When the cost of the retreat came into view, objections careened inside my brain like bumper cars at the boardwalk. It was way out of my price range. I couldn't possibly take the time off work. I hadn't been on a horse in years. I didn't want to go by myself. Hunched over my keyboard, weighed down by my doubts, I was relieved to hear Damon's voice calling me from downstairs.

"Jeri, what are you doing? I can't get my printer to work, dammit! Can you come here and check it out?"

I clicked off the website and started for the stairs.

Two days later I found myself back at the Gathering the Soul website. Transfixed, I read, "During the week we will ride horses, leaving our civilized world behind. Come because you want to experience 'The Last Best Place.' Come because you love horses. Come because your soul is calling you to go deeper."

Goose bumps spread over my arms, and my hand jerked up to cover my mouth.

There it was in words, right in front of my face! How much clearer did it have to be? My soul *was* calling me. I sat back in the chair and waited. I waited for myself to talk me out of it again, but that didn't happen. Instead, I watched myself get up and walk to my purse to retrieve my credit card. As if being led by some remote-controlled gadget out in the universe, I entered the number into the computer and clicked Submit. Only then did the thought explode in my head like fireworks: I'm going to Montana! Hell, yeah! I'm doing this!

Connie, that elusive woman who appeared to me in a magazine ad, magically jumped off the page when I opened my email inbox the next day: "Dear Jeri, Welcome to an exploration of what forgotten, lost, or neglected parts of your own soul you will discover and reclaim at the Gathering the Soul Retreat." A shiver shook me. Was it excitement? Was it fear?

On a Sunday in August, seven months from the day I signed up, I walked with my suitcase through the rural, almost deserted, airport in Great Falls, Montana. When I stepped through the glass doors to find the van that would take me to the ranch, a hot wind whipped my hair, tossing it around my face. A piece of newspaper rolled through the empty parking lot like a tumbleweed. There was no van, and the only other person on the sidewalk was a rail-thin man with a stubbly white beard, smoking a cigarette. I felt like a little kid who has raced to get to the circus, only to discover that it left town the day before. I let out a jagged sigh and turned to go back inside.

Peering around the baggage claim, I saw a couple of women talking near the other exit door. They looked kind of like me: middle-aged, wearing colorful, casual clothes. One had a backpack looped over her shoulder. I rubbed the base of my neck, gripped my suitcase and walked toward them. When I was in talking distance, I introduced myself and in the same breath asked if they were going to the Blacktail for the Gathering the Soul retreat. I let out a short, shrill laugh of relief when they answered yes.

The transport van finally arrived, and I climbed in to the bench seat at the very back for the one-hour ride. Gazing out at the big blue sky dotted with enormous white clouds, I spotted a red-tailed hawk gliding along beside us. My whole body went soft, as if I had swallowed one of those puffy, marshmallow-like clouds. In that moment I wasn't at all nervous about not knowing what lay ahead of me in this distant land that was entirely new.

We turned off the two-lane highway onto a winding, pitted dirt road. The van slung up a swirl of dust when it stopped in front of a large rustic two-story log cabin.

"We're here, gals!" the driver called out.

One by one we grabbed our suitcases and ambled into the lodge. The smell of food greeted us, along with friendly faces and a small border collie that bolted over to me, wagging her tail.

I glanced around the homey, knotty-pine dining hall and recognized Connie. She stood up and crossed the room to us. She was wearing a pink-and-beige-checked cowgirl shirt, and she was slender, probably in her mid-sixties, with touches of blonde in her otherwise gray hair.

"Hi, I'm Connie," she said softly, nodding to us with a slight smile. "Welcome to the Blacktail." She emanated an alluring calmness that helped me feel relaxed. I liked her right away.

I sat down at our table with my plate of food and listened to Connie go over our schedule for the next six days. We were to meet at nine o'clock in the hogan, a structure close to the lodge, to share messages from our dreams and to journey, a kind of guided meditation, to find our power animal and our unique gifts. All of the rides would be in the afternoon. She explained that each of us would be paired up with a horse for the week for what she called a "Horse as Mirror" exercise.

"A horse responds to a person like a mirror," she said. "As you stay conscious of your thoughts, feelings and sensory perceptions while interacting with your horse, you can learn about yourself. Bring your journals on all of our rides so you can write down your reflections."

To cut costs, I had opted to share a room. My roommate was Diana, one of the women I had met at the airport. After we both used the bathroom down the hall, I turned out the light, and as moonlight flowed across the floor, covering everything in a soft, silver glow, I slipped into a deep, exhausted sleep.

I awoke to the sound of thunder. Sitting up with my eyes wide open, I realized it was dawn. Listening more intently to the endless pounding, I thought, That can't be thunder!

I jumped out of bed and ran over to the window. Horses were galloping past, being herded to the corral after roaming the ranch all night, dust swirling up from their hooves.

Suddenly I was returned to my childhood, bouncing bareback on Pixie. I imagined gripping her mane and hugging her strong, wide body as tightly as I could with my legs. I closed my eyes and reveled in the memory. When I opened them, the last horses were passing. I lingered at the window until all was silent again. Then I turned and tiptoed back to my warm bed.

Several hours later I walked alongside the other women through a golden meadow toward the first morning session of Gathering the Soul. I followed the path to the hogan, an octagonal wooden cabin amid miles of grass, stones and sky. One of the women placed her hand on the door and pushed. I closed my eyes for a moment and let out a sigh before stepping inside. Light streamed through the huge picture windows that surrounded Connie, who sat on the floor in the middle of a circle of empty BackJack floor chairs.

"Please join me," she said. "If you would like, take a rattle or drum and then find your place for our ceremonial opening ritual."

I picked up a rattle and settled next to Diana, someone familiar. I wasn't really sure what to do, but I knew that I wanted to do it right. I kept my eyes open the whole time. My thoughts tugged at me: What am I supposed to feel? Am I feeling it? What will I say when I introduce myself to the group?

As the sounds of our rattling subsided, Connie spoke again. "Today we will explore an ancient healing practice called journeying to discover your power animal. Indigenous cultures for thousands of years have believed that each one of us has an assigned power animal that has always been protecting us. Close your eyes, take a deep breath, relax and allow me to guide you with the drum and my voice to find your power animal."

I had heard of totem animals before, but I didn't really know what they were. Was that what we were going to do, find our totem? Was a power animal the same thing? I shifted from side to side, trying to get comfortable with so little between me and the hard wooden floor. Connie's drum sounded. I shut my darting eyes and thought, What if I'm the only one in the group that doesn't find my power animal?

Connie's slow, hypnotic voice floated along in cadence with the drum. "You are walking on a path in the forest.

Feel your feet landing on the earth. Use all of your senses to be there. What do you hear? Perhaps birds singing in the trees. What do you see? Is it a warm day? Do you feel breezes on your face?"

The rhythmic drumbeat somehow transported me, and within minutes I was walking along a path in DeLaveaga Park, a forest near my house. It was a warm day, the sky was blue and the wind rustled the leaves in the trees as I passed by.

Connie continued. "As you walk on your path, you see the opening of a cave. Keep walking toward the cave and go inside."

I saw the cave. It was a large black hole in the side of a hill just ahead of me. I walked up and, as instructed, went inside.

"You see light at the end of the cave. Walk toward the light."

There it was, the light illuminating my way through the darkness.

"When you get to the opening, step to the other side and ask for your power animal to come to you."

I climbed through the hole. I was standing in a beautiful meadow surrounded by redwood trees. I ran through the meadow, entered the cool, shady forest and stepped onto a soft dirt path lined with bright green ferns and patches of ivy. I could hear small animals scurrying behind rocks and tree trunks. Are you my power animal? I asked, but no animals appeared to me.

I walked on through the forest until I came to a clearing. There I looked up and saw a hawk circling above me in the crystal-blue sky. The same feeling washed through me that had reassured me the day before when I saw the red-tailed hawk; I was not afraid of being in unknown territory. A bolt of joy followed as I stared up at Hawk through the hot rays of the afternoon sun. In that moment I knew my power animal was Hawk.

The drumming grew faster. "It is time to come back now. Thank your power animal for being your ally and helping spirit. Return on the path the same way you traveled in."

Moments later I opened my eyes and wiggled my toes. I was relieved to have found my power animal. Even more, I was enchanted to discover that I could travel to another place that felt so real—a dimension I later learned was a spirit realm in non-ordinary reality.

After we shared our power animal journeys, the women at the retreat started calling me Hawk Woman. This felt right, though I didn't know why. In the years since the retreat I have come to understand how Hawk helps me nurture my intuition and gives me a vision of my life from a broader perspective. Hawk shows me that I have the strength and insights to follow my visions with grace and agility, riding currents of wind in a gentle sky.

THAT AFTERNOON WE WERE going to meet our horses and begin the horse-as-mirror exercise. I ran up to my room after lunch and pulled on my Ariat boots, which I had bought especially for this trip. I rushed, almost skipping, toward the corral, where I hoisted myself up on the worn wooden fence and looked out at the saddled horses, the same ones I had watched galloping that morning. Surely I would know which one was mine, especially after my experience with the hawk.

The wrangler was talking with Connie on the far side of the corral. He looked my way, nodded and walked toward me. I jumped down off the fence and waited. Excitement spun around me as each of the other women met her horse.

When the wrangler reached me, he wiped his hand on his pants, held it out to me and said, "Howdy, I'm Bruce."

As I shook the proffered hand, I watched his brow squeeze into rolls of wrinkles. Something was wrong.

"Jett," he said, "the horse you were going to ride this week, isn't here. He didn't come in with our roundup this morning. I imagine he's spooked by the young mountain lion that's been stalking the ranch for the past couple of days."

The energy that had filled me since the morning's journey drained away, and I took a step backward. "Will ... will he come back?" I stammered. A flush of heat ran up the nape of my neck. I had traveled all this way for a transformative experience, and now my horse was a no-show. When I had watched the horses run by that morning, my horse was not among them. He hadn't bothered to return to meet me. How could this be happening?

"Most likely he'll be here tomorrow," Bruce said. "Let's get you on a horse today so you can ride out with your group."

I climbed onto the back of my substitute horse and for forty-five minutes tried to adjust to the hard, unforgiving leather saddle as we rode up a winding mountain trail. When we got to the overlook that revealed the breathtaking beauty of the vast countryside, I squashed what could have been an awe-inspiring moment by thinking, If Jett is my mirror, am I spooked like he is? What am I afraid of?

THE NEXT AFTERNOON as I approached the corral, Bruce waved me over. He was saddling up a white horse with large black and brown spots. I gasped. Jett resembled Mickey!

"Ms. Jeri, he made it back," Bruce said.

"Yes, he did," I replied, slowly walking over to Jett and wrapping my arms around his soft neck. Cheek to cheek, we stood together under the pale blue sky as if nothing else existed, until Bruce's voice cut through the silence.

"Well, Ms. Jeri, it looks like you're very happy to see Jett."

"You have no idea, Bruce."

Smiling, I dropped my arms and strolled around Jett, as Connie had instructed us to do for our horse-as-mirror assignment. She told us to look for clues from our horse that might help us learn something about ourselves. I noticed that Jett had small scrapes all over his body.

Bruce was right there, cinching up Jett's saddle, so I asked, "What are those marks?"

"Oh, he has scars from running through bushes and getting caught up in barbed-wire fences," the wrangler replied.

Though I stood very still, a flurry of questions whirled in my mind. Do I have scars like Jett? I wondered. Am I wounded? Am I in pain? Why don't I feel it?

"Well, Ms. Jeri. He's ready to ride," Bruce said to me with a half smile.

I put my foot in the dangling stirrup, pulled myself up on Jett's waiting back and took my place in line. Jett followed the other horses like the obedient animal he was trained to be. He put his head down and plodded along.

It didn't take me long to see myself in the mirror of Jett. For years I had walked in silence. I worked hard and did what I was told, what I was trained to do, believing that my accomplishments assured me approval and acceptance from others so that I would be loved. Feeling the sway of Jett's gait underneath my body eased my troubled mind, but I still was unsettled.

That night in the hogan, Connie wrapped up the evening by saying, "We will meet here again at nine in the morning to begin sharing stories about your sacred childhood wounds."

Panicked thoughts galloped through my mind. Had I missed something when I read the ad about the retreat? I had arrived at Blacktail Ranch with visions of me riding horses through the Montana countryside with other women, carefree, chatting and laughing. I had imagined campfires, wading barefoot across a creek and writing inspirational messages about nature's beauty in my journal. I had neither read nor imagined anything about sharing childhood wounds.

I followed the thumping of my heart across the meadow toward the lodge, barely looking at Connie or the other women. Along with my horror at the prospect of sharing childhood wounds, I was surprised by my own reaction. After all, my childhood happened a long time ago. I wasn't wounded. I had a successful career, family, friends and good health. My life was in order.

THE NEXT MORNING in the hogan, the moment came when I was the only one who had not spoken.

"So, who still has to share her story?" Connie asked. No one said a word.

I sat in the silence, feeling the knot in my stomach twist. Heaving in a breath, I finally said, "It's my turn, Connie."

"Okay, Jeri. When you're ready, please begin."

In that moment a powerful compulsion took control of me, and I was myself as a little girl. These words tumbled from my eight-year-old mouth: "I walked outside the house onto the cement porch. My daddy was yelling at my mommy. They were standing really close together in the yard. Their words were loud and scary. My mommy pushed my daddy into the sticker bushes. He stumbled back but then stood up and hit my mommy in her face really hard with his fists. She fell. I screamed 'Mommy, Mommy' and ran to her."

Between sobs I continued. "Daddy told my sister to bring a towel from the kitchen. There was blood on my mommy's face. Daddy put the towel around her face and helped her back into the house."

I told them how we put our mom in the car and drove her to the hospital, where she got stitches. "The next day and the day after I was afraid to look at my mommy because her eyes were so swollen she looked like a monster."

Everyone in the room was crying.

I wiped my wet cheeks with my sleeve, took a long, ragged breath and said, "There's more. My father could never hold down a regular job. He was in and out of jail until he was sentenced to life without parole in 1984 for drug trafficking. My sister and I are the loves of his life. I only see him in the visiting room of a federal prison. It's been that way for thirty years."

This was the first time I admitted to anyone that as a child I had seen my dad hit my mom. Over the years my mom and I had talked about the abuse, but I had never brought it up with my dad or anyone else. I didn't see how it could help me, and I certainly didn't think it would help my relationship with my dad. I didn't want to hurt him. After all, he was in prison. Wasn't that enough for him to deal with? Until that day in Montana, I had no idea that my fear, shame and grief from witnessing domestic violence as a child and from having a father in prison were very much alive inside me.

WE WERE SCHEDULED for a sunset ride that evening. I found Jett tied up and waiting for me at the corral. I went out into the cool country evening on Jett's strong back, my body shaking like the earth in the aftershocks of an earthquake. Surrounded by big pink sky, listening to the sounds of women chatting and laughing on the trail ahead of me, I realized that I had exposed my deepest pain to others and to myself and lived through it. Was it coincidence that I was now magically riding a horse in the exquisite, nurturing beauty of Montana, or did my soul's healing have something to do with all of this?

As we headed back to the corral, the sky burst into bright orange and purple. Connie galloped up to me on her spirited

Me riding Jett in Montana.

black horse, the one in the magazine ad, looked me straight in the eye and said, "Jeri, stay in the question." Then she galloped away.

Mesmerized, I watched her ride into the sunset, just like in a movie. I instantly knew what she meant. She was telling me to continue to be curious, to ask more questions about my wounds, to follow my soul now that I had allowed it to show me parts of myself that were unexplored and neglected.

There was still more to come.

On the sixth and final day of our retreat, Connie arranged for us to climb down into the depths of a sacred Native American cave that was located on the property. During our check-in meeting the night before she had explained, "Inside the cave I'm going to lead you in an ancient Native American healing ritual. You will go with your power animal on a journey to discover your unique gift."

It was close to a hundred degrees that day. Under the sweltering summer sun we walked the three miles to the mountainside cave site. It was a relief to follow Connie down into the cool darkness of the ancient Native site, where we settled on large boulders arranged in a semicircle. Connie began our ritual with drumming and chanting. We joined in.

Following Connie's guided suggestions as she drummed, I closed my eyes and dropped into a state of deep relaxation. I was standing on a grassy cliff overlooking the ocean, wearing a white cotton blouse and a long white billowing cotton skirt. My power animal, the hawk, flew down and landed right next to me. I climbed on his back and we flew off the cliff together, seeking my unique gift. My hawk and I traveled all the way around the world. I could see below me the landscape and peoples of India, Russia, China and many other lands. I whispered to myself, "Take me to my unique gift. Show me a sign when I have found it." To my surprise, my hawk brought me right back to where I had started my journey, standing on the grassy cliff. I climbed off his back and he flew away.

Did I find my unique gift? I wondered. Had I missed something or failed to understand?

Connie's drumming grew softer and gradually ceased. She asked us to share what we had experienced. "Did you find your gift?" she asked.

A couple of the women told us what they had discovered. I had nothing to share. I wanted out of the cold cave and back to the warm air outside.

Connie asked us to start singing a song, any song. “Singing,” she explained, “opens doors between the worlds, creating sound vibrations that will invite in our helping spirit teachers and ancestors for healing and guidance.”

I didn’t want to sing a song.

I was fighting my desire to leave the cave when I was overtaken by the urge to sing “Over the Rainbow.” I only knew one verse, and I was sure I would sound silly, so I ignored my urge.

At that moment, my body started to shake, and without me willing it, I began to sing softly. To my delight the rest of the women joined in. They knew all the verses. I followed along, humming when I didn’t know the words. The cave filled with the sound of our singing.

The song ended. There was a period of silence as we gathered our belongings, climbed out of the cave, shivering from the cold, and resurfaced into the warm light. Bruce had a table set up for us under the ponderosa pines with all kinds of wonderful food for our last supper together. He had brought along his guitar and sang rough-and-tumble cowboy songs as we ate, talked and laughed.

“Okay, gals. I got time to sing one more song before we have to pack up and head on back,” Bruce said, an easy smile brightening his rugged face.

He strummed his guitar and to my astonishment started singing “Over the Rainbow.” Every fiber of my body responded as tears welled in my eyes and rolled down my flushed cheeks. In that moment I knew a benevolent force was trying to tell me something. I wasn't sure what the message was, but I suspected it had something to do with finding my unique gift. I went to bed that night with a profound feeling of satisfaction growing inside me.

THE NEXT MORNING, the last of the retreat, I went to find Jett. I walked alone to the corral, and there he was, tied to the fence. I placed my hand on his forehead and said, "Jett, thank you for being my friend here in Montana and carrying me steadily one step at a time toward knowing my soul." Once again tears welled up as I gazed into Jett's big brown eyes. I realized that I could feel more, that I was less afraid of my emotions.

An hour later we piled back into the van with our suitcases. As we drove I gazed out at the countryside. A red-tailed hawk glided high above us and I smiled a deep smile. I was now Hawk Woman, growing into the wildness and the freedom that name implied. I was starting to trust the connection between me and the vast landscape of my life, like a hawk looking down, surveying everything from high in the sky as a curious observer.

20

Daddy Oz

In October 2011 I traveled to Atlanta to visit my father at the prison and to share with him my adventures and insights in Montana.

I had never told him how his rages frightened me when I was a child. I had never told him how much sadness and disappointment I felt about him being in prison. I lived year after year minimizing, covering up and stuffing my feelings deep inside me with controlling thoughts like "Oh, it's not that big a deal. It doesn't really matter. It's okay." Having experienced the power of my inner strength and courage in Montana, I knew being honest and speaking up was an important next step to healing my relationship with my father.

The first day I visited Dad on my own so he and I could talk. Lyn planned to come with me the next day because Dad so loved seeing his two-both together.

Even though it was early in the morning, the noise rose to a roar as more and more visitors met with their imprisoned loved ones. At last the steel gates opened and Dad walked into the room. We rushed up to one another, as always, and hugged, and, as always, I felt that familiar comfort in his arms. As we sat down, I reflected how this man, our father, still had a sharp mind, a fit body and a zeal for living, even after spending close to thirty years in prison, surviving serious health issues and transitioning to a new prison as an elderly inmate.

His radiant face showed that he sensed my excitement. "I can't wait to hear about your trip to Montana," he said. "I'm ready. Tell me, Ber."

Starting from the beginning, I told him about seeing the ad in the magazine, flying to Montana by myself, bunking with other women and riding horses every day. Unlike most of our visits, when he talked nonstop, Dad watched me the whole time, smiling, not saying a word. He reminded me of a little kid listening to a bedtime story. I told him everything, from going on a journey to find my power animal, Hawk, to flying with Hawk from the sacred cave to find my unique gift.

When I got to the part in the hogan when we shared about our childhood wounds, I paused and dropped my head. I could not yet tell him exactly what I said about seeing him hit my mother, but I went on.

"Mom was so scared of you that she left. When she did, my security went with her. I had to leave my house, my friends, my school. That was really hard for me, Dad. When she came back, you went to prison."

I looked up at him and said, "Dad, I didn't realize how hurt I was."

Dad's face got serious. His eyes squinted a bit, and his mouth became tight and drawn. He looked back at me with tears in his eyes. "I knew you were hurt," he said.

We both fell silent and cried together. Something happened in that tender, powerful moment that changed me forever. At last I was being real and vulnerable. I didn't have to pretend anymore that everything was all right. I was setting myself free to love and accept my father fully just as he was. I opened my heart, and when I did, I gave my father's love somewhere to go inside of me.

I sensed that same feeling, that benevolent force guiding me, that I felt when I heard Bruce sing "Over the Rainbow." I went on telling my story. I told Dad about my uncontrollable urge to sing "Over the Rainbow" in the cave, then described how the wrangler sang it after we came out of the cave and the profound effect that had on me.

"Dad, do you want to hear the song?" I asked. "I know all of the words now."

He looked at me with his soft brown eyes and nodded. He was so entranced by my story that he didn't speak.

Against the backdrop of all the noise in that visiting room, Dad heard me sing, verse by verse, every word to what has remained for me a sacred song. As I sang, Dad and I sat together, holding hands, while our souls were transported to that special, peaceful place where skies are blue, where troubles melt like lemon drops, and where dreams that you dare to dream really do come true.

Dad never stopped trying to get out of prison. Between 1984 and 2011 he appealed his case twice, applied once for compassionate release, and applied for a presidential pardon and geriatric parole. He spent countless hours in the prison library reading legal texts and recruited fellow inmates with legal skills to help him.

In 2012 Dad submitted a motion to the courts outlining why his sentence was illegal and requesting re-sentencing that would include a provision for parole. Lyn and I wrote letters of support. We so wanted to get our aging father out of prison and into a more supportive and comfortable place where we, his family, could take care of him.

We waited for more than three months. Then a moment of hope. A United States district court judge agreed to review his re-sentencing motion.

As we waited for the judge's ruling, Lyn came home one day to discover a card on her door from a federal caseworker, asking her to please call. The caseworker told my sister that she needed to schedule a site visit at her home so the worker could confirm the conditions where Dad would be living if and when he was paroled were acceptable. She told Lyn that after the site review, it would take three to four months for Dad's paperwork to get through the system.

We were elated. Did this mean Dad was getting out? Could it be that our father was not going to die in prison?

I wrote to Dad.

Dad, you always amaze me … talk about being a fighter! You just never gave up on getting out and now it looks like our dream is coming true. Your grandkids are waiting for you. I've been telling all my friends that you are getting out. Everyone is so excited! They keep saying be sure and tell me when you know the date he is being released. I'll come to Atlanta to see you that day walking out a free man.

His email response to me was this:

At last my rainbow dream is coming true. I sat in my room with tears in my eyes and my heart aching. After 30 years I will be with my daughters to walk with them holding their hands ... I love you so much and finally I am going to be able to really be with you and not in one of these prison rooms.

On June 22, 2012, Dad received the judge's decision. The eleven-page judgment gave detailed rebuttal to the points made in his petition for parole, stating, "The court is without authority to re-sentence under the former Rule 35 (a) since the sentence imposed was not illegal. Petitioner's Motion to Correct an illegal sentence under Federal Rule of Criminal Procedure 35 (a) [Doc. 158] is DENIED."

Dad would not be released from jail.

Lyn called and told me the bad news. I was stunned.

"How was Dad when you saw him Saturday during your visit?" I asked.

"Oh, he's trying to put on a good face, but I can tell he's upset and sad about the news."

"And you? How are you?" I asked Lyn.

"The same as he is. Why would they send a parole officer to my house to interview me if he wasn't getting out?"

YET EVEN WITH this discouraging news, I felt that we were stronger than ever in spirit. Since the day I told Dad about my Montana trip and sang "Over the Rainbow" to him, I was not the only one who was discovering and reclaiming the neglected parts of my soul. I sensed that my father was too. Almost every email, letter and phone call we shared was enlivened and inspired by the new role he had assigned himself, Daddy Oz.

> *December 2011*
>
> *It is so fitting for us to understand the life forces of our rainbow land that you found for us in Montana. Yes, we understand the universe of energy from the great sun of life. I like thinking about our cells magically converting sunlight to energy. Every living thing starts from that cell that grows into life. It is Lyn and Jeri. And love. Our purpose is to know more about love. What do you think? Daddy Oz.*

> *February 2012*
>
> *I am so proud of my daughters. It really is great to be a daddy to girls. I love you, honey ber. Sending a big hug and Daddy-Oz love. See you over the rainbow! Bye for now.*

December 2012

From Santa Oz in Emerald City far away into the rainbows and love. I see happy girls with their red slippers flying around!!! There is Toto and Daddy Ber WOW!!!!!!!!!!!!!!!!!! What a good time we will have being together in this beautiful land with pretty rainbows high in the sky where blue birds fly and there is Hawk. Merry Christmas to our Ozies. Oh boy we will be the happiest munchkins in the whole universe. Sending big hugs from the green Santa with red shoes on. Daddy

I was surprised by Dad's vivid imagination and how he put his visions into words. He easily transported himself beyond bars to beautiful lands over the rainbow, where he was free to walk with his daughters. And while the experiences were transitory, in those moments he was hopeful. He was devoted more than ever to exploring how we could be together, nourished by the strength of our love.

The more I opened myself to my father, the more unanswered questions I had. Yet the unknown seemed less frightening to me. When I stayed in the question, another piece of the puzzle would arrive and help me heal. In 2013 I enrolled in a yearlong life-coach training program. My vision and purpose for myself was changing. I wanted to know how to have a better, more authentic life, and I wanted that for others.

While in the program, I discovered Byron Katie, whose method, The Work, now informs my whole life. From her book *Loving What Is*, I learned there is *what happened* and

Sol, Dad, me, Jessica and Lyn at USP Atlanta. Dad was 82.

there is *what I made up in my own mind about what happened.* I learned that my judging thoughts, not the situation, kept pain and confusion alive inside me, even years after the situation was over.

During my life-coach internship, a master coach helped me free myself from the thought I wrote down on a worksheet, about when I was ten and my father went to jail: "My father shouldn't have been a criminal and left me to go to jail." For years I had blamed my father for abandoning me, which made me the victim of my story. It was true that my father went to jail when I was ten. As a child I interpreted this to mean that he didn't love me, because if he did he wouldn't do things that could put him in jail away from me.

One of the techniques in The Work that disrupts and defuses untrue thoughts is turning the thought around from the person you are blaming to yourself. I turned "my dad left me" around to "I left him." With that reversal came a profound realization. For years I had distanced myself from my father with my judgmental thoughts. I had imprisoned myself in the jail of my mind, unable to love my father fully because I had left him. His going to jail had nothing to do with him not loving me. I also realized that I had not only left my father, but had also left myself. I had buried my compassionate self with fearful thoughts that closed me off to love, not only for my father but for me.

The healing process that had begun in Montana was heightened by doing The Work. When the judgments faded, in their place I found empathy for Dad and for me.

Lyn, Dad and me at USP Atlanta.

21

Zero to Hero

In 2014, at the age of 82, Dad submitted a compassionate release petition to the warden. Compassionate release is early release for compelling reasons, such as when the defendant is suffering from terminal illness, from a permanent physical or medical condition, or from deteriorating physical or mental health due to aging.

I watched my dad grow old in prison and longed to have him with me for his remaining years. I wanted to take care of him. When I was hiking on the forest trails, I envisioned him there with me. My every hope was that something would work to bring him home.

Two major events gave Dad more hope than ever before that he might have a chance to get out. On August 5, 2013, *USA Today* published an article entitled "Holder Revamps Prison Policies: Seeks to Curb Minimum Sentences." In a speech before the American Bar Association, Attorney General Eric

Holder stated that he was pushing for early release for seniors and ill inmates who no longer posed a danger to society.

The other remarkable event was "The Untold Story," which Dad spent weeks writing for my sister and me. His story recounted in detail how in 1960, when he had his bail bonding company, he saved Dr. Martin Luther King Jr.'s life.

ALTHOUGH I HAD NOT heard about Dad's involvement with Dr. King before, I did know that our father was one of the first white owners of a bonding business in Atlanta to hire a black man in his company. I had met Rogers Hornsby when I was a child, but I didn't understand then that when my dad hired him, black people were prohibited from eating at restaurants in the South, they were banned from public parks and they had to sit at the back of the bus.

Years later, while visiting Dad in prison, I pointed out that hiring Rogers was a big deal back then. I asked him why he did that. Dad didn't really talk much about the past or tell stories unless you asked him.

He paused for a moment. "I hired him because he was the right man for the job," he said at last, "and hiring him was the right thing to do."

Then he told me some details from his childhood that I had never heard before.

"Do you remember I told you that when I was born I wasn't breathing and almost died until I was revived by the doctor?" he said. "I was a sickly, weak kid after that. I was allergic to just about everything. When I was a baby,

I had to wear aluminum cups tied to my wrists to prevent me from scratching my eczema. That's the reason we moved from Pennsylvania to the South. My doctors told Grandma and Grandpa that a warmer climate would be better for my health."

But Dad's family soon learned it wasn't easy for a Jewish family to find housing in the South in the late 1930s. When they finally did settle somewhere, a cross was burned in their yard, and a note inscribed in blood red ink was nailed to the door: "Jews are not welcome in this neighborhood."

Dad had told me a portion of this story years earlier when I asked him why, when I was around five years old, he changed our last name from Rosenthal to Ross (he changed his back again went he had a business venture, Rosenthal & Son, with his father).

He said, "I didn't want you and Lyn to endure the prejudice I endured growing up."

The first day he entered the hallways at Bass High School in Atlanta, Georgia, he was targeted as a weakling, a Jew kid, the kind of kid that excited the vicious pack of school bullies. One sweltering day they surrounded him out in the dusty schoolyard. He couldn't escape. Jerry Jerome, the leader, pushed my father as the rest of the boys yelled out, "You sissy Jew boy, little Harry Rosy."

Jerry punched my father again and again. Blood streamed from Dad's face as he tried to protect himself by holding his arms around his head. My dad didn't fight back. He didn't have the strength. He just kept begging Jerry to stop. When Jerry finally did, Dad stumbled home, ashamed and crying.

"When I was sixteen I started taking boxing lessons at the local YMCA," Dad said to me. "I told your grandma that I was taking swimming lessons. I knew she would try to stop me from boxing because of my asthma. My coaches saw fighting talent in me and worked hard to help me get strong. At the boxing matches, people watching would yell, 'Kill the Jew.' That made me madder and I would hit harder. I won every fight I was in."

Dad went on to tell me that he named me after that bully. He said, "I didn't want to ever forget that day Jerry Jerome beat me. I wanted to remember so I would never ever again be that weakling, not able to fight back."

By reading old newspaper articles in a scrapbook my grandma had put together, I discovered that Dad had earned the title of Southeastern Golden Gloves lightweight boxing champion. He learned early on that he had what it took to be a fierce competitor in the ring and in the streets. Fighting became a way of life for my father.

According to Dad's "Untold Story" and confirmed through other sources, on October 19, 1960, Martin Luther King Jr. and many others were arrested during a sit-in at an Atlanta restaurant. Most were released, but a previous sentence for a minor traffic violation provided an excuse to hold King, and he was transferred to Reidsville state prison in southern Georgia and sentenced to serve time. In the middle of the night he was chained to the floor of a van and taken to the prison where, Dad said, he would surely have been killed, because the prison was run by the Ku Klux Klan. Dad made some calls, asked for some favors and after eight days was successful in posting King's appeal bond. He arranged for a private plane to pick him up and bring him to the DeKalb County courthouse.

Here is Dad's account of that momentous day.

> Around 5 p.m., the courthouse was flooded with news media and TV reporters. Two deputies escorted King into the sheriff's office. I was there waiting for Dr. King to sign the bond. As he put down the pen after signing, he looked me in the eyes with his hand extended out to mine and said, "Thank you Mr. Ross. I know this wasn't easy to do, but you did it. I will always be grateful to you." He turned to walk out into the crowd of people. Camera bulbs were flashing and popping.

I couldn't help thinking that "The Untold Story" was a vivid example of embellishment. Could our father possibly have saved Martin Luther King's life?

DURING ONE OF THEIR fifteen-minute phone calls, Dad told Lyn, "Go see Lonnie King and give him 'The Untold Story.' He has influence in Atlanta. He could go with you to see Congressman John Lewis."

Lonnie C. King Jr. was the leader of the Atlanta civil rights student movement in the 1960s. Although he was no relation to Martin Luther King, he marched beside him as one of his closest friends and fellow activists. With great generosity of spirit, Lonnie King went with Lyn to see Dad at the penitentiary, and he agreed to go with my sister to pay a visit to Congressman John Lewis to ask him what could be done to get Dad out.

Lonnie told us, "Your dad was the only bondsman that helped us students when we would get arrested for protesting. He didn't have to do that. I want to do what I can to help him."

Louise Hornsby, practicing attorney and former city court judge, also went to see Congressman Lewis on Dad's behalf. Her husband, Rogers, was the African American man Dad had hired in the early 1960s when he needed a job. Louise credited my father for giving Rogers a job that helped provide financial support for both her and her daughter to attend law school and become attorneys.

Lonnie King, along with Reverend Wyatt Tee Walker, a national civil rights leader, theologian and cultural historian, and two other civil rights leaders, Reverend Otis Moss Jr. and Reverend C.T. Vivian, wrote a letter to President Obama and Attorney General Holder, confirming that Dad was instrumental in helping the civil rights movement.

February 14, 2014

Dear Mr. President,

We are writing you regarding Mr. Harold Rosenthal, inmate number 08075-020, who is being held at the Federal Penitentiary on McDonald

Boulevard in Southeast Atlanta. Mr. Rosenthal is seeking a compassionate release parole and with this letter we are seeking mercy and compassion for Mr. Rosenthal in hopes that his parole be granted. During a time of great racial upheaval, Mr. Rosenthal stood up for us and hundreds of other young college students and adults by providing the bonding as we challenged the system of segregation in Atlanta. At a time when it was dangerous to stand up for Civil and Human Rights, he stood up for us.

We believe that in his current state, we who were beneficiaries of his actions need to now stand up for him. He is gravely ill and has served 30 years without parole for his actions. Therefore we are appealing to you to use whatever power you have to release Mr. Rosenthal for humanitarian and health reasons. We do not believe at 83, he will be engaged in any activity that would offend the moral and criminal code of this great country as he approaches the sunset of his life.

In the 1960s, Mr. Rosenthal was the owner of the Fulton Bonding Company and was instrumental in posting bond for all of us, as we serially challenged the system of total segregation that pervaded all of Atlanta, the entire South and many portions of the mid-west.

In addition, in October of 1960, he also provided the bail for Dr. Martin Luther King Jr., who was probably targeted for death when he was whisked

> *in the dead of night from DeKalb County, Georgia, to the prison of Reidsville, Georgia, which is located in one of the most racist portions of the State. We sincerely believed that if Dr. King had been compelled to stay incarcerated in Reidsville, he would not have survived.*
>
> *Soon after Mr. Rosenthal posted the bail for Dr. King, the Chief of Police of Atlanta, Herbert Jenkins, moved to revoke his bonding license. This was a rank case of discrimination based upon the fact that Mr. Rosenthal is Jewish …*
>
> *With the deteriorating physical and mental health of Mr. Rosenthal, the rising cost of elderly care, and the fact that some elderly inmates have already been released under medical reprieve, we ask that you release Mr. Rosenthal to the care of his daughter, Lyn Ross, in Atlanta, Georgia, where he can be appropriately cared for at this time in his life.*

Not only was I impressed at what these civil rights icons had said about our father, including their confirmation of "The Untold Story"; I was also struck by the fact that after more than thirty years in prison, Dad's warrior spirit, his heart of a giant, still inspired him to make connections with important people on the outside, people who cared about him enough to write to the President of the United States.

Seven months later, a letter from Reverend Walker arrived in my sister's mailbox. He had been chief of staff for Dr. Martin Luther King Jr. and was a former executive director of the Southern Christian Leadership Conference. His letter, or what seemed to be a chapter in a book he was writing, was entitled "Why the First Attempt on Dr. King's Life Failed." My sister scanned it and sent it to me. I opened the document and read:

> The planned assassination was clear. Dr. King was to be killed in Reidsville during a prison disturbance. It was hoped to be characterized as "accidental" to mask the real execution. However, this sick plan was blown wide open due to the diligence of Harold Rosenthal in securing bail for Dr. King. Rosenthal was "owed" by many people in his role as bondsman, and at great risk to himself and his company, with courage and determination, he secured bail for Martin Luther King to free him from Reidsville Penitentiary in South Georgia.
>
> Had King been assassinated in Reidsville, there would not have been a successful Freedom Ride, stand-off at Albany, the confrontation at Birmingham, the March for Selma, the march on Washington, or the Nobel Peace Prize. Harold Rosenthal is literally an unsung hero of the Civil Rights Movement.

I was struck by the fact that Dad didn't have to do any of it. He didn't have to bail out the students. He didn't have to hire a black man to work for him. He didn't have to get involved with Dr. King's release from Reidsville. But he did.

When Dad finally called and I had a chance to talk to him about the letter, I was brimming with excitement.

"Dad, Dad! You changed history! You saved Dr. King's life!"

I BELIEVED THAT this positive turn of events indicated that Dad's karma was changing because he was changing. He had helped me with our business venture, and he was learning more about the transformative powers of love. Now he was being celebrated for the work he had done for the African American community during the civil rights movement.

Over the phone he said to me, "I just want my girls to be proud of me. I've gone from a zero to a hero in your eyes, and that means more to me than getting out of prison."

22

Forgiveness

I believe that my father suffered from a mental health condition called Intermittent Explosive Disorder (IED). I didn't know about IED until I began to question how my father landed in prison for life. Dad had been incarcerated for thirty years when I finally conducted some preliminary research into rage disorders.

IED is characterized by repeated episodes of aggressive, impulsive and violent behaviors that are entirely out of proportion to the situation. Often these outbursts result in the person assaulting others and destroying property. Mostly men have IED—often men who have been raised in families in which explosive behaviors, including physical and verbal abuse, are common. Risk factors include a history of head and brain trauma.

This condition is said to affect more than ten million Americans. People suffering from it are not able to control their rage, which comes on without provocation and has devastating consequences for them and everyone in their lives. Not surprisingly, IED is frequently a factor contributing to incarceration.

My mother had told me many times that when Grandma was giving birth to Dad, she hemorrhaged and almost died. My father also was in peril: he was born blue and not breathing. The medical team was able to revive him, but for approximately five minutes no oxygen was going to his brain. Mom is convinced that Dad suffered brain trauma that ultimately caused him to have organic brain damage.

"Your dad could have done anything, been anyone. He was incredibly intelligent, but he had a deficiency. I see it so clearly now. When we were married, he changed jobs again and again. He struggled to fit in and be successful at a straight job. But he just wasn't cut out for the nine-to-five sort of life. He would get so stressed that he would break out in hives all over his body. He was trying to handle his family responsibilities, but the pressure was more than he could take. He expressed his frustration and anger just like his grandfather Max."

Dad was greatly influenced by Grandpa Max. "Max managed to accumulate wealth by being forceful and dishonest," Mom said. "He was a con-artist salesman, and he would tell anyone anything to get their money. He revered money as a way to manipulate and influence people in order to get what he wanted.

"Max was a tyrant with a raging temper. He carried a baseball bat in the back seat of his car. If someone made him angry while he was driving, he would jump out at a stoplight, wave his bat in the air and cuss at them. He was married and divorced six times.

"Both your dad's father, Grandpa Bert, and Max were salesmen who tried to help your dad by hiring him in their construction companies, like when I met him in Jacksonville. But pretty soon your dad wasn't able to stick with those jobs. When Harold was arrested and then went to prison in Reidsville, well, that's when Bert's drinking got much worse."

Hearing about Great-Grandpa Max helped me understand better how Dad came to be the man that he was. Not many years ago I learned that even after decades in prison, where he took a type of anti-anxiety medication that he jokingly called "Gorilla Biscuits," Dad still had rages. He never told me about them, but when I asked RV, one of his friends inside, to tell me about Dad's life in prison, this is one of the stories I received:

> I met Harold in 2001 at USP Leavenworth. I had just begun my sentence, and Harold had been in prison for seventeen years. He was one of the respected older convicts, so it was a pleasure and an honor to get to know him.
>
> One time, Harold was having trouble in the legal room. I went in to see what was going on. Harold ended up so mad that he cussed me out. Now, Harold had cussed me out a hundred times before, but that time was bad. That night I couldn't sleep thinking about it. Well, the next day,

> Harold walked up with tears in his eyes and gave me a big hug and told me how much he loved me. I was so relieved that I hadn't lost my friend. After that, when he got mad he would always give me a kiss on top of my head and tell me he was all right, that this was just something he had to go through.

I wasn't trying to make excuses for Dad, but learning about IED sure helped me see him in a more forgiving light.

THE NEXT TIME I visited Dad at USP Atlanta, fueled by my budding honesty and forthrightness, I looked him straight in the eye and said, "Dad, you have a rage disorder."

His eyes got wide. He sat back in his chair and said, "I have that." It was clear that, in all his life, no one had ever connected his uncontrollable outbursts to a mental disorder.

"I know, Dad," I said. "And that disorder could partly explain why you struggled to hold down a regular job and wound up incarcerated."

That exchange with my father helped me make my next decision. When I finished writing the chapter in this memoir about everything I had said in the hogan in Montana three years earlier, I sent it to him. I wasn't expecting or needing an apology. I learned from Byron Katie that when you hold on to needing an apology, you're held hostage to stressful thinking about what someone else has to do in order for you to feel better. I was taking responsibility for my own happiness and peace of mind no matter what my dad did or didn't do.

I wasn't sure why I felt compelled to send him the chapter until I got this letter from him a week later.

> *When I read your letter I cried and felt terrible. That is what I did to Mother Joan. It sure hurt me and I know Joan. Please tell her I am sorry. I was terribly wrong. I know all the apologies will not take away the scars to your mother and to you.*

When I shared Dad's response with Mom, she wrote this to him:

> *It's true that there were deep scars for a long time, but after years of reflection, I have since fully forgiven you and have long since experienced complete healing of my psyche. I believe your remorse and apology are sincere since I know the soft side of your heart as well.*

When I read these words, I let them sink in to every bit of myself. I sighed, and when I released breath from my lungs it covered the land and sea with waves of tranquility. I sent this email message to Dad:

> *I knew it would be hard for you to read my Montana story. I didn't want you to have to feel*

sad or bad, but what I now know about love is that sharing our feelings honestly is the only way we can mend souls. Through this journey we have more room to love, have compassion and can have more joy!! You are with me on the sacred path because you understand what that means ... your daughters are really proud of you! Love ... your Hawk

The more courage I had to face my wounds and communicate what I honestly felt, the more my dad did too. We had reconnected so much by now that I trusted myself to be vulnerable with him, and I knew that he felt the same way about me.

23

Daddy Tree

Unexplainable things were happening for reasons I didn't fully understand. As I said, the more I stayed in the question and followed my inner compass, the more I trusted signals and messages that nudged me toward discovering my unencumbered, true self. I realized that I didn't have to explain these messages, but I did have to pay attention when I received them.

I was at Moe's Alley, a dark, sultry jazz club in downtown Santa Cruz, one Friday night when I got another nudge.

Dr. Susan Allison and I had been friends for several years. I had read her books and knew that, as a transpersonal psychologist, she used healing modalities including shamanic journeying. After a drink and thirty minutes shaking myself wildly on the dance floor, I found myself standing next to Sue on the outdoor patio.

Since Montana, I had been intrigued by the idea of learning more about shamanic journeying, but I did not anticipate what happened next. Much as I had been unable to stop myself from singing "Over the Rainbow" in that sacred ancestral cave, as I stood next to Sue on the patio I blurted, "Hey, Sue. I want to be your apprentice and learn more about shamanic journeying and spirit realms. What do you think about that?"

She smiled. "I think that's a great idea," she said. "When would you like to get started?"

DURING MY YEARLONG apprenticeship with Sue, I learned that shamanism is a spiritual practice that dates back tens of thousands of years to indigenous cultures all over the world. Shamanism teaches that all living things—people, the earth, trees and animals—have souls, and all souls are energetically interconnected. There has recently been a resurgence of shamanism as a pathway toward self and community healing, a path that can be followed by anyone seeking a deeper connection to the meaning of the lived experience.

Journeying is a core ritual of shamanism that opens a portal to the subconscious. When journeyers listen to the repetitive sounds of a drum or rattle, their brain waves slow down into theta, a meditative trance-like state, which helps the journeyers dissociate from linear time and space, ordinary reality and logical thinking in order to access empowering messages from their own soul and from all the collective souls in the web of life.

Shamanic journeys start with an intention. Enlightening messages typically come through metaphor and images instead of in words. For example, Hawk appeared to me in my first journey in Montana, sharing the feeling of flying free and encouraging me to seek a vision for my life from a higher perspective. Until that day I didn't believe in anything that I couldn't see with my own eyes and understand with my rational mind.

Now, as I worked with Sue, I sought to learn as much as I could about loving my father, myself and all of life. When I walked into Sue's office for the first time, I was nervous, but I knew there was no turning back. I wanted to know what my next journey would rouse in me.

I stated my intention out loud: "I want to learn from Hawk how to heal and align with my soul's wisdom."

I closed my eyes, and listened to Sue's voice and recorded drumming. Within a few moments I was walking on a familiar trail in the Carmel Valley mountains. When I emerged from the forest, I found myself looking out over a canyon. Hawk came to me and I got on his back. As we were soaring along in the sky, I transformed. I shapeshifted. I became Hawk.

A powerful feeling of freedom overcame me as I flew through the canyon, seeing with Hawk's laser vision the fish in the stream below. I was guided by the scent of the earth while the wind under my wings held me up. As Hawk, I didn't know what was going to happen next, and I didn't care. I was present in the moment. I glided alongside the stream until it became a roaring waterfall. I then flew back to where my journey began, overlooking the canyon. Sue guided me to thank Hawk before I transitioned into my own body, returned to the room and opened my eyes.

I was astounded, just as when I had journeyed in Montana, at how real it felt to fly with Hawk and, in this journey, to become Hawk. Sue explained that my power animal was showing me how to know greater levels of trust and safety.

"In childhood, when we experience chaos and trauma," she told me, "we believe that we have to raise ourselves. We lose trust that anyone else will. We feel unsafe. Essentially, Hawk was showing you that you can let go and trust that the wind will hold you safely in the sky. Instead of trying to grip on and control your life out of fear, you glided along the stream, a metaphor showing you how to flow in your life with ease, releasing control even when you don't know exactly where you're going." She encouraged me to continue my journeying practice.

As I left Sue's office that day, I knew that my awareness and perception of reality had changed. I had been on a spiritual quest for years, reading self-help books and attending workshops, but it wasn't until I experienced shamanic journeying that I finally *felt* what I would call spirit or my own soul. I had the comforting feeling that I was finally home.

In the weeks following my session with Sue, I practiced shamanic journeying, learning more and more and opening to the wisdom and guidance of my soul.

Here's another recounting of a journey I took.

November 2014
Intention: Ancient Grandmother Teacher,
help me know my father.

We sat around a fire where the silhouettes of others were writhing with the beat of the drum, creating a force in the middle of the circle. I could see inside the circle and it went way down into vast sprays of colored mist. Grandmother told me to throw in my fears and doubts, to let them burn away in this circle of depth, the abyss. I started to feel lighter and freer, less afraid. Then I fell into the abyss. My legs were flailing. But then I bounced up, like I had been caught in a safety net. When I fell again and bounced up, I could see that I was being caught and tossed back up by a huge pair of hands that I knew were God's hands. I relaxed and let go. I asked my Ancient Grandmother Teacher, "How is this helping me to know my father?" She said, "He is being caught by these same hands. It is not all for you to do."

After several months of journeying, one misty morning I was walking with my dog in DeLaveaga Forest. I had an urge to find a special tree that I would call my daddy tree. I walked along the soft dirt path until a huge redwood rose on the side of a steep hill in front of me. I stopped and took it in. It wasn't the largest tree, it didn't have the longest, lushest branches, but there it stood, still strong after hundreds of years, surviving storms, droughts and fires.

That's how I felt about my dad. He was a survivor, like this tree.

I approached, wrapped my arms around the trunk and laid my face on the soft furry moss of my daddy's chest. Waves of sadness shook my body, like the gusts of wind that shook the broken branches above my head, and I cried hard, like a downpour in a summer storm. Ten minutes later I felt better. As I had learned in Montana, I could be sad and it wouldn't break me. My daddy tree's roots held me strong and solid on the earth. His branches showed me how to reach high toward the infinite sky.

When I told Dad about my daddy tree, he understood immediately. He began to encourage a connection with me by mentioning the tree often in his emails and letters.

> *To our Ozie Hawk for life and love and everlasting in the universe of Oz land.*
>
> *Your daddy Oz sure enjoys the life given to him with his two daughters. Sissy loves you so much. You are great honey. We are a proud family with our kids and grandkids. Keep up your strength for them. They are your life here and in to the great beyond. We are not divided. All one. Each one of us belongs to the other in spirit and love. Our hearts are strong and love forever. Sending a big Daddy Tree Hug.*

When Lyn came to visit me, we hiked together through the forest to our daddy tree. She wrote him this letter:

February 2015

Hey Daddy Oz … I went to the Daddy tree and we sent you green healing love energy … love particles. Did you feel it? I put my hands on the mossy bark, looked up to those tippy-top branches and sent all of my energy from the ground, through my body, out my arms and into that old tree. Do you know what happened next? The wind came along and the branches started moving and shaking! It looked like they were waving to me. Love Lyn

Just as our father wanted, his two-both, my sister and I, were growing closer together because of my spiritual awakening to the soul in all things. My healing was her healing, just as I had experienced with Dad. Before we hiked out of the forest that day, for the first time I noticed two smaller redwood trees, just down the hill from the daddy tree, that had fused together at the base of their trunks.

"Look, Lyn!" I exclaimed. "There we are—the Lyn and Jeri trees!"

We laughed wildly, just like when we were little girls running through the kudzu on a balmy summer eve in Decatur, Georgia.

Before I left for Atlanta to visit Dad in the spring of 2015, I journeyed, with his permission, to find his protective power animal guide.

May 10, 2015
My intention for this journey:
Find Dad's power animal

I started with deep breathing. It felt like my body was breathing itself.

I was on my path at the mountain's edge.

I then experienced Dad's transformation into a black panther, his body and his face with bright yellow eyes. I was with him, he walking beside me in the jungle as panther. He climbed to the top of a tree and slept there. His panther-ness exuded the energetic emotions of strength of body, confidence, belonging and power. As panther he could have complete trust that without struggle, without fear, with no need for control, he was safe in his space and place in the universe.

When I came back to my path, panther came with me. We walked out to the ledge and looked out at the canyon below. The world and its blessings filled our hearts.

On May 29 I was with Dad in the visiting room at USP Atlanta. I couldn't wait to share some of my journeys with him. I was especially excited about the journey in which I found his power animal, black panther.

"Panther really fits you, Dad," I said. "When I researched, I learned that panthers are powerful animals that walk alone. They are so strong mentally and physically that nothing can stop them from getting what they need. They represent bravery and self-reliance."

He said, "Yeah, I see that is like me."

I told him how much I loved it when, after he transformed into the panther, he returned with me and sat with me as we looked out at the vast canyon. He got tears in his eyes. I had been noticing how Dad's eyes filled with tears more as he aged and as we grew closer. He was more easily moved by emotion. So was I.

"Dad, you told me that all we need to do is learn more about love and that you wanted to be with your girls forever over the rainbow. We can do that!" I exclaimed.

Dad asked me how journeying had changed me.

"When I explore with curiosity the messages from my journeys, I'm going beyond the mind, beyond thought," I told him. "I finally feel like I'm connected to my soul as my guide, that I can trust that I have help. I'm not alone. I've spent so much of my life trying to control and make things happen, avoiding my emotions and not being honest with myself. I built little bars around my heart because I didn't trust. I started not trusting when I was a child."

He sat back and said, "Ber, I know it's been rough." He took my hand, looked in my teary eyes and asked me, "But would you change anything?"

I paused for a long moment, feeling an incredible rush of what I can only describe as pure tenderness. A tear fell down my cheek. I looked at my eighty-four-year-old father, who had been incarcerated for thirty-one years, and said, "No. Nothing."

And this is what he told me back: "I think that if we changed anything, we wouldn't be where we are right now."

Me at USP Atlanta with Daddy Oz when he was 85.

In that present moment we sat together in silence, holding hands, knowing the same truth. Through and because of the pain, the struggle and the sacrifice, we were exactly where we needed to be, loving one another and loving what is. In my mind I pictured Red in *Shawshank Redemption* walking up to Andy on that beach in Zihuatanejo.

After the visit, we wrote to each other.

August 2015

From Dad to me: *This is the love message you sent me on the back of our black panther that loves you so much honey daughter of mine. Your message is so strong and beautiful, its eyes glowing and happy ... You shine in the sunlight and you glow in the dark ... Being your black panther, I really love it, me on 4 paws. Like a real cat. I like that. I can see you next to me and we can walk into the sky. Bye for now honey. Your daddy of love. Me.*

From me to Dad: *Keep dreaming of OZ land, daddy! I will travel there to meet you. I can in spirit realms. All things are possible! Your soul will guide you and reunite you with the source of all things. Our bodies were never made to last forever ... We all do our best. It's not perfect, but again it was not meant to be. Love you forever, Ber.*

24

Soul's Journey

I had conversations with my father about death. Shamanism had taught me that death was a kind of transformation, not an end but the continuation of the soul's journey. My dad was old. His death was imminent. As his time neared, I believed that I could use what I was learning to help him make the transition.

I did not expect my beloved husband to die before my father.

In November 2015, Damon and I were vacationing with Lyn and Tom on the island of Saint Martin in the Caribbean. Lyn's marriage to Eric had been short-lived and ended in divorce. She met and became engaged to Tom in 2003. Damon and Tom were like brothers, and the four of us loved traveling all over the world together.

While we were in Saint Martin, Damon developed a nasty, persistent cough. When we got back to California, he saw several doctors, was told that he had gastrointestinal issues and was treated for them. The cough persisted, though, and he was sent to a pulmonologist, who diagnosed stage 3 lung cancer. We were devastated, but we got busy with daily radiation and weekly chemo to shrink the tumor in hopes he could have surgery.

In September 2016 we learned that Damon was no longer a candidate for surgery because his cancer had spread to his adrenal gland.

After the radiologist gave us the news, I walked outside the building, called my mom and wept as I told her, "I'm losing my husband." Mom and I cried together while Damon was inside having his final radiation treatment.

For the next seven months we fought his cancer. By April 2017, however, he was so weak that I talked to him about going to hospice. That was a tearful day for both of us, but he agreed. During the three months he was in hospice, we grew closer. Often while he rested he would listen to the sounds of my gentle drumming as I journeyed, with our dog sleeping next to the sofa bed.

DURING THOSE MONTHS, my journeying brought me the comfort of my soul's messages. This is one of my journeys:

> *Hawk flew me to my place of power. There I inhaled a purifying herb like sage that made me fall unconscious. My limp body was placed in the cave of my Ancient Grandmother Teacher where she and*

others of my tribe performed a ceremonial soul healing for me.

When I awoke, my Ancient Grandmother Teacher asked me, "Are you afraid of Damon's dying?"

"Yes. It is so hard," I said, running into her arms.

She held me and said, "If that is how you want to tell that story, you can call it hard. Does it have to be? Damon's life was never meant to be permanent. No one's is. Is that what you believed it was?"

I felt myself relax in her arms. And I released my fear. I accepted that I had been gripping onto something that never was meant to be.

On July 15, 2017, Damon passed into spirit.
This is my journey five days after my beloved transitioned:

I buried my to-do list in the earth and flew with Hawk over the vast sea to my place of power. When I landed in my tree of life I sensed a great welcoming. I felt an immense belonging and love as if the land and trees, the sunlight, and wind were all comforting me.

I climbed down the tree, unable to resist the pull of this natural world. As I lay in the cool stream, I melted into the soft water. While I didn't hear Damon's voice or see him, I felt him in the water, the stones, the leaves. I glanced up and saw my Ancient Grandmother Teacher standing on the cliff. I ran to her and she embraced me with a smile.

"Where is Damon?" I asked her.

"He is in your heart. His soul is merging with yours. Speak the universal language that is love and exude that love with all whom you meet. Let them feel his soul shine through you."

A month after Damon's memorial, I was on a plane to Atlanta. Over the years, when faced with formidable events in our lives, my sister and I traveled to be with our dad no matter where he was. Now I needed to feel the comfort of his love after Damon's passing, and I knew that he needed to see me to know that I was strong enough to go on.

When at last we were together, Dad looked into my eyes. "Are you okay, baby girl?" he asked me.

"Dad, I'm not okay," I told him, "but I'm doing the best I can."

25

Sunlight

In September 2017, a month after I returned to California, Dad's second compassionate release petition was denied.

He pushed on, despite hands gnarled with arthritis, most of his teeth broken off at the root, and a frame that had shrunk from five foot eight to my height of five foot three. His once-handsome face, with its distinct jaw line, was caved in, and I had noticed during my visit that he repeated himself more than he had done in the past. He didn't seem to hear what I was saying, partly because of the noise in the visiting room, but also because his mind was slipping.

That October, just after his eighty-sixth birthday, Dad was diagnosed with aortic valve disease, in which the opening between the heart and the body's main artery (the aorta) stops functioning properly. Lyn told me that within a matter of weeks his legs swelled up so much that he could hardly walk.

He had shortness of breath, no energy and little appetite. As well, he developed a prolapsed esophagus, which made eating almost impossible. The fellows in the prison supported him under his arms to help him walk, pushed him around in a wheelchair, brought him special food that was easier for him to eat, and helped him out to the yard every once in a while so he could sit in the sun.

He never missed a visit with Lyn, but he was determined not to let her see him in a wheelchair. She found out from one of his inmate helpers that Dad told them to wheel him up to the visiting room door, pull him out of the wheelchair, stand him up and push the door open. Lyn would watch him waddle over to where she was sitting. Unable to bend his swollen knees, he would turn around and drop into the chair next to her.

My kids were very concerned about him, as we all were. From the research I had done online, I knew that aortic valve surgery could fix his heart valve. Would his age preclude him? Would the prison staff approve the surgery?

On Christmas Eve, I was in the kitchen pulling apple pies out of the oven when forty-year-old Chavo said to me, "Grandpa should get the surgery to help him and stop the suffering. All I ever wanted was to sit down with him one day and have a nice dinner together. Here we are having one more Christmas without him."

As I put the pies on the counter, I had the painful thought that death also would stop Dad's suffering. And when Dad died, wouldn't he finally be out of prison? I was keenly aware that, as his family, we had no say in his fate.

Two weeks later we found out that Dad was denied the surgery because of his age. Was it truly because of the risk, I wondered, or was it the cost?

Six months passed before I could get back to Atlanta to see my father. On June 3, 2018, I mailed this letter to him, five days before I would board a plane to visit him in USP Atlanta.

> *Hello Dear Daddy of Mine,*
>
> *I found this passage and read it to Lyn as I'm packing my suitcase for traveling like Hawk through the sky to meet you.*
>
> *The panther renews and transforms the life of the rain forest. Panther stands for sudden transformation, life and death. It might seem odd to us that the transforming force in the universe is also associated with death, yet to the ancient Americans these two energies were cut from the same cloth. That which endured was always changing and renewing itself.*
>
> *I'll be there soon! I love you with all of my heart and soul,*
>
> *Ber*

Finally, on June 9, 2018, I was with my sister, driving to USP Atlanta. She pulled into the parking lot and we stared up at the hundred-year-old gray building that jutted out of the earth like a massive stone statue. It was a summer Saturday. That meant longer lines. We used to visit Dad on Fridays, but the administration had removed the Friday visit option a couple of months earlier.

I looked. Sure enough, there was the line.

I breathed. "It's okay, Jeri," I told myself, as I did at the start of every prison visit. "Just relax and be patient. There's nothing you can do." I depended on my wise words to myself to help me with whatever awaited me inside.

"Your coming is lifting his spirits," Lyn told me.

I opened the car door and was engulfed by the Georgia humidity. We were going to have a sweaty wait until we could get inside. I was walking around the car to put my purse in the trunk when a movement in the sky stopped me. A hawk swooped down and landed on a nearby telephone pole.

"Look, Lyn! It's a hawk!" I exclaimed. My body vibrated with the excitement I always felt when I saw my power animal. That hawk was an omen, a message that opened my heart to the moment.

"Wow. That's a trip," she said with a smile.

Before she snapped the trunk shut, her cell phone rang. It was Dad.

"We're here, Dad," she said. "We just saw a hawk." She paused while he talked, then said, "We'll be there soon."

"The hawk lives here," she told me, putting her phone back in her purse in the trunk. "It's always flying around the prison yard."

Goose bumps broke out over my arms.

TWENTY MINUTES LATER, the line hadn't moved. Thirty minutes after that, the thick, smudged glass door to the prison buzzed, and the first ten people in line pushed inside.

Lyn was number ten. She motioned me to squeeze against the wall so the door could shut behind me. I stood in a small tight pack of women like me, who knew not to wear revealing clothing, like leggings or sheer white or sleeveless shirts; no khaki pants, which were too similar to the inmates' clothing; no jackets with zippers that would set off the metal detector.

Twenty more minutes passed.

A baby cried. His mother cradled him in her arms, along with a plastic bag holding a couple of diapers and some change for the vending machines. "God, come on," she said, rolling her eyes.

There was only one person on the desk. Someone new. When she finally called my name, I slipped off my shoes and put them in a bin on the security conveyor belt, which already held several other pairs. I watched the bin move through the machine. The floor felt sticky under my bare feet. I walked through the metal detector, slipped my shoes back on when they reappeared, and held out my hand to be stamped. The steel gate buzzed open, and our small group followed the guard down a red brick hallway to the elevator.

We ascended three floors and walked down another hallway to a steel gate. "Almost there," I said to myself. The final gate slid open, releasing the deafening noise of people shouting in the visiting room. My heart pounded. I looked for Dad in his usual spot. He wasn't there.

The guard motioned us to take a seat. At last, after ten minutes, I caught sight of Dad looking disheveled and confused. His head was down. As I always did, I ran up to him for our customary hug, but he walked right past me to the big metal garbage can. He bent over it and vomited.

I put my arm around his back and helped him into the plastic chair to keep him from falling on the floor. He collapsed into me. I pulled his head to my shoulder and held him. He pushed his body as close to mine as possible, resting in my embrace, while Lyn stared at us with tears in her eyes. I was alarmed at his frail state and shortness of breath.

"What's wrong, Dad?" I asked, stroking the back of his neck.

"I have pain in my chest," he said, grimacing. "Get me a Coke."

Lyn headed for the vending machines.

"How long have you been feeling like this?" I asked, raising my voice to compete with the noise all around us in the visiting room.

"About an hour," he said.

All the time Lyn and I had stood waiting in line to see him, he had been trying to hold on so he could come out to see us.

He reached into his top pocket and put a nitro heart pill in his mouth. Lyn handed him the Coke. He took a sip but couldn't swallow. Lyn grabbed the garbage can and pulled it closer. He vomited again.

He dropped into me and whispered, "I love you two so much."

"Dad, it's okay," I said, holding my hand on his chest. "Maybe you should go back."

He nodded yes.

I got up and spoke to the guard, but fifteen minutes later no one had come with a wheelchair.

Suddenly I felt him tense. "I can't breathe," he mumbled and slumped over, attempting to lie down on the row of plastic chairs. I thought he was having a heart attack. Lyn jumped up and went to tell the guards that he needed help.

The guard on the desk picked up her phone, while the floor guard shouted over the noise in the room, "We have a medical emergency! All the inmates must get up and move to the far wall!"

The room got quiet. Everyone turned to look at the guard and search the room for the source of the emergency, but no one got up. He shouted again and the men reluctantly stood and walked to the end of the room. At last a guard appeared with a wheelchair, heaved Dad into it, twirled him around and rushed him out of the room.

Wait! I screamed to myself. Aren't you going to hug me goodbye?

It took me a long time to get a breath down to completely fill my lungs, and even longer to make my way out with Lyn. The whole visit had gone so terribly wrong. And Dad was so sick. What was going to happen to him?

For the rest of the day I tried to put Dad out of mind. Over the years I had gotten good at that. But when I was alone in bed that night, I put a hand towel around my face to catch my tears and sobbed.

Lyn called the prison the next day. No answer. Federal rules prohibit communication about inmates, but she called anyway. For two days we had no idea what had happened to Dad.

Then Lyn asked a friend of Dad's who had recently been released if he could find out anything from the inmates he knew inside. She learned that Dad was in the hospital, and he wasn't doing well.

In spite of the grim news, I was relieved to learn that Dad was in the hospital. I wanted to be with him, to care for him, but at least he must be getting competent care. I had planned to visit him the next weekend, while I was still in Atlanta, but the days passed with no further word. I had no choice but to go home to California, three thousand miles away from my gravely ill father. I felt so helpless.

Two weeks later we still hadn't heard anything from Dad or the prison officials. As each day passed, I wondered if Dad was dead or dying. There was no way to know.

Early one morning I was sitting at my desk when my home phone rang. "United States Government" flashed on the caller ID. A telemarketer, I thought, and almost didn't answer.

"Hello."

"Are you Ms. Jeri Ross?"

"Yes, I am."

"I'm Ms. Whitely, calling from the Atlanta federal prison. I'm Mr. Rosenthal's case manager."

Not once in all the thirty-four years my dad had been incarcerated had I received a call from the prison. I blinked rapidly and waited for what was coming next.

"I tried to reach your sister, Lyn Ross, but I only have her work number. I didn't leave a message for her there."

"Oh, oh, I can help you. What do you want to tell us?"

"I'm calling to arrange for you to see Mr. Rosenthal in the hospital."

"You, you're calling to tell me I can visit him?" I stammered. It took me a moment to grasp what she had said. "Oh, that's great!" I paused, thinking hard. "I wish I could," I said. "I'm already back in California, but I'm sure my sister will want to see him. We haven't heard anything in over two weeks."

I gave Ms. Whitely Lyn's cell number. Within minutes, Lyn called me.

We were both relieved but unsure of what exactly was happening. Dad had been in the intensive care unit for a week. He hadn't suffered a heart attack but was feeling the effects of the blockage in his heart and the inability to eat due to the collapse of his esophagus.

Ms. Whitely called on a Wednesday. She told Lyn to send her an email to request a hospital visit for the upcoming Saturday. In the meantime, Chavo and Jessica took the first flight they could get to Atlanta. I was conflicted about staying home, but I had to take care of my mom, who was recovering from a minor surgery. Sol had a new baby, so he stayed home too. I was proud of Chavo and Jessica for their love and kindness, for wanting to be there for the family.

They sent me cell phone photos of their visit. Dad could barely talk, but he did find the energy to communicate with the kids and Lyn. Lyn and my daughter massaged lotion into his dry hands and feet. Lyn even played him his favorite music from our childhood over her cell phone: Mario Lanza, the opera singer.

Dad was in a long-term-care medical center that was charged with doing all it could to rehabilitate the patients. They gave Dad IV fluids, Ensure meal-replacement drinks and oxygen; they tried to get him up to sit in a chair. Aside from the arthritis in his back and neck, he didn't seem to be in pain.

We were conflicted about these efforts to revive Dad. From my journeys with spirit, I felt that Dad was dying. When Lyn asked him directly, he said that he wanted to die.

On July 10, a week after Chavo and Jessica came home, I traveled to Atlanta.

I walked into the hospital room with Lyn, and there was Dad sleeping with an oxygen mask on his face. If it weren't for the two burly guards sitting along the far wall of the room watching TV, it would have been no different than visiting any elderly dying person in the hospital. After years of living with the fear that our dad would die in prison, here we were with Dad dying in a hospital, just like most old people. That thought helped me adjust to the sight of my father's diminished figure.

"Dad," I said softly, hoping to rouse him.

He opened his eyes and gazed at me with a blank stare. He didn't smile. He didn't reach out to hug me. Did he even know it was me?

"Jeri came from California to see you," Lyn said sweetly.

He nodded, a slight movement. I leaned over and kissed him on his forehead, the only place I could reach, since the oxygen mask covered most of his face. Handcuffs dangled from the side of the bed.

A nurse came with a thermometer. "I have to take your temperature, Mr. Rosenthal."

Dad turned his head toward the wall as she put the device under his arm.

"He was getting pretty ornery with me yesterday," she said with a half smile.

"What happened?" I asked.

"Well, he's feeling better today. Yesterday he was cussing at me to leave him alone. He said he wanted to die."

"Oh," I said. I wanted to shout, Just leave him alone! Let him have some peace!

When she was gone, Lyn slipped off the oxygen mask. "Dad, I'm going to clean your face. Would you like that?" she asked.

Again that tiny nod. I held his hand, the same hand that through the years he had reached out to hold mine, while Lyn wiped the chocolate Ensure from the hairs of his gray beard.

I jumped when a loud beeping burst from the side of the bed. A nurse came charging into the room.

"You can't take that mask off," she said. She replaced the mask while we stood there with only half of his face cleaned. Another nurse came in with a tray of food.

"Is he eating?" I asked.

"Oh. He ate a few bites of his eggs this morning."

I asked what was in the IV.

"It's fluids with vitamins," she said.

From my experience with Damon, I knew that hospice could help Dad pass in peace with dignity, providing whatever would make him most comfortable, such as morphine, instead of forcing his body to stay alive with liquid nutrients.

Lyn interrupted my gloomy mood. "Hey, Dad," she said brightly. "We're going to sing 'Over the Rainbow.' I have the music here on my phone."

She cued up the song. We both leaned over him. I was so overcome with emotion I couldn't sing. When the song ended, and I gained some composure, I whispered into his ear, "Dad, just let go. We're all going to be fine. I'll take really good care of Lyn."

For the third time, that slight nod.

I sensed that he wanted something more, more reassurance, more peace.

His eyes were closed. I pulled up a chair and sat on one side of him, while Lyn stood on the other.

"Dad, I'm going to tell you a story. Would you like that?" I paused and collected myself. "Remember, we've been preparing for this for a while now. I'll help you with my story."

His nod was a bit stronger this time.

I began.

"We are on a path in the jungle, you, me and Lyn. Hear the birds in the trees. Feel the freshness of the green plants and trees all around us. Look, here comes your black panther. See his shiny black fur and bright yellow eyes. He is asking us to follow him on the path. He is leading us into a cave. But it is not dark. Rainbow crystals fill the cave with colorful light that shines on us and goes inside our bodies. We feel safe and happy. Panther motions us to follow him through the cave. We step through the opening at the end of the cave. Our bodies rise in the dark air and we are floating in a sea of soft waves that hold us and rock us. Our bodies are light and translucent as we float together where there is no thought, no fear, nothing to do and nowhere to go."

I continued. "Dad, let go and feel the soft, gentle rhythm as we float up, up, up to the rainbow. Up, up, up to the rainbow."

Dad nodded again. He knew what I was saying. He was with us.

A WEEK LATER we were on our way for another visit to be with Dad in the hospital. My goal for the day was to hold sacred space, to create white loving light for my father's comfort. I had resigned myself to his imminent death and even wanted him to go so his suffering would end. At the same time, I didn't want my dad to leave me. I didn't want his death to be real.

As Lyn drove us through Atlanta traffic, I stared out the window at the gray city sky, wondering how I was going to brighten up Dad's spirit when my light was so dim.

I walked into the sterile, hot, stuffy hospital room and my light got even dimmer. Dad was slouched over to one side of the bed. The staff had pulled the blankets off his body and removed his socks, revealing his white, peeling feet, which were held to the bed with metal shackles.

My heart sank. Seeing the shackles around his ankles forced me back to the painful realization that my father was in custody and that he wasn't dying in a hospital like any other elderly man. I held back my tears and touched his arm. He barely opened his eyes. He didn't speak exactly, but mumbled sounds that didn't make sense to us.

Lyn and I spent three hours with Dad that day, doing whatever we could to help him be more comfortable. We gave him water, put his Ensure on ice so it might feel better in his mouth, asked the staff to move him into a more comfortable position, talked to the guards about why no one from the prison had come to see Dad. We asked the nurses to replace the huge breathing mask with a smaller one, and we rubbed his body and crusted lips with lotion.

All the while I grew more and more agitated that Dad was being kept alive to suffer. He still was receiving IV fluids, Ensure and oxygen, but no medication to ease his transition; nurses were constantly coming in to take his vitals; machines continually buzzed and beeped.

I fell into bed at nine that night, exhausted.

On our way to the hospital the next morning, we talked about how Dad had slipped through the cracks. The prison doctor had told us he didn't have the authority to make medical decisions about Dad. He said we had to speak to the physician at the hospital. We told the prison doctor that Dad needed hospice care. He agreed, but only six federal facilities offered hospice, and all were far away and had no available space. Dad was too ill to move anyway. Federal prisons were packed with old-timers, like Dad, who got long sentences in the eighties.

Dread and hopelessness filled me as my sister and I sat in slow-moving traffic. When we arrived at the hospital, we found Dad in the same condition as the day before. The only change was that they had tied his arms to his sides so he couldn't pull off his oxygen mask or IV tube. He mumbled and tried to reach for his face. I moved closer to the bed so the guards couldn't see me unfasten the tie and make it longer—long enough so Dad could rub his face.

An hour later I went down the hall to use the restroom. When I returned, I was greeted by a young woman with a row of keys dangling from her belt. She thrust out her hand and grasped mine. "Hello, I'm Garcia," she said. "I'm here from USP Atlanta to see how Mr. Rosenthal is doing. I know him well."

"It's great to see you," I said, feeling a sense of relief that someone from the prison administration had finally come to check on our father.

Dad opened his eyes at the sound of her voice.

The woman went over to his bedside and said, "How are you, Mr. Rosenthal?"

Dad stared at her without saying a word.

"Hey, everyone is asking about you. Did you know you were famous?" she said, smiling.

While Dad didn't have many friends and family on the outside, during the seven years he was incarcerated at USP Atlanta, he had acquired a network of men who functioned as his inside family. Garcia told us that for months the guys had been watching out for Dad; they were always by his side with whatever he needed.

"What do you want me to tell them?" she asked.

Dad could only speak in a whisper, but he managed to make himself understood: "Tell them I see great strength in them. Tell them to stay strong."

He smiled and shrugged his shoulders.

"Well, Mr. Rosenthal, I surely will tell them what you said. I have to go now."

Lyn and I followed Garcia out to the hall.

"This hospital is mandated to rehabilitate patients," Lyn said. She told Garcia about all of the measures that were in place to prolong Dad's life when what he needed was hospice.

Garcia nodded. "It just so happens that I'm having a staff meeting with the warden in the morning," she said. "I'll tell him about Mr. Rosenthal."

When she reached out her hand to say goodbye, Lyn grabbed it and pulled Garcia closer to her. Lyn's body shook as she cried on the officer's shoulder. When Lyn finally let go, she said, "We need your help. I'm hopeful that you'll be able to help our dad."

AN HOUR LATER it was time for me to say goodbye. I sensed that this was the final moment I would physically be with our dad. Lyn was right beside me.

We leaned over and heard him whisper his last words to his two-both. "My two beautiful daughters," he said. We each kissed him. Then we walked hand in hand to the car, tears rolling down our faces.

The next morning, while I lay in the cozy bed in my sister's guest room, I pulled out my headset and listened to the recorded drumming I had on shuffle. The intention for my journey was to check in with Dad's soul and ask for a message from him.

In my journey, a huge red velvet curtain drew back to reveal Dad with a big grin on his face in a two-level houseboat. An angel, sitting on a red leather cushion, was steering the boat through waves of clouds in the wide-open sky. As I watched, instead of feeling sad and distraught about my dying father, I was filled with happiness. I realized that Dad was still showing me a positive way through life, leading me with his love and strength into the next chapter, on his way to a glorious afterlife over the rainbow.

I left the next day to go home to California.

My sister continued to advocate for Dad's comfort in his final days. Two weeks after I left, he was diagnosed with pneumonia and transferred to ICU for still more lifesaving care. No matter his condition, the prison's orders that the hospital rehabilitate him didn't change. We begged them to let him pass in peace, with medication to relieve his pain, but because he was in a private hospital, the prison medical staff continued to tell my sister that they didn't have the authority to make decisions for Dad's care. Our dad was in limbo between these two jurisdictions.

After eight weeks in the hospital he had lost so much weight that regular-sized shackles slipped off his bone-thin ankles. Instead, his ankles were attached to the bed with cuffs made from plastic cable ties. As if, in his condition, Dad might try to escape. It was ludicrous, but he was the property of the Federal Bureau of Prisons, and it was the law that Inmate #08075-020 be secured at all times.

Finally, in frustration, Lyn cornered a doctor who miraculously appeared in the ICU to check Dad's vitals. She looked him straight in the eye and said, "Tell me, do you see his condition? Do you really think he's going to get up out of that bed and go back to his prison cell?"

The doctor held her gaze. "No, ma'am, I don't," he said. He told my sister that he would check with Dad's primary-care doctor.

When Lyn went to see Dad the following afternoon, the same doctor told her that if it was the family's wishes they would start administering lorazepam and morphine to control his blood pressure. At last he was going to get the care he needed. They were helping him let go in peace.

The next day, August 3, 2018, a nurse from the hospital called Lyn around ten at night.

"Ms. Ross, please come to the hospital immediately. There has been a change with your father," she told Lyn.

Lyn knew right away what she meant. Our dad had died. But Lyn didn't have the warden's approval to visit that night, so she was afraid she would be turned away.

"Please tell me," she asked the nurse. "Were you in the room with him when he passed?"

"Yes, ma'am."

"Could you describe that moment for me?"

"I would like to let you know that your father's last breath was peaceful," the nurse said, her voice soft.

"Thank you. That's all I need to know," my sister told her and ended the call.

Moments later, my phone rang. Lyn told me that our father had passed. A stillness came over me.

I quietly said to my sister, "I love you, Lyn. You did such a good job with him. We can be grateful that he is no longer suffering."

I went to bed and awoke the next morning drowsy and somber. I got up and walked to my computer. On my screen I had put up a yellow sticky note, retrieved from the many letters stored in a crate in my office, and read, *Love you so much ... my baby Ber ... You're sure a good girl ... I am so proud of you. DAD*

No one loved me the way my dad did.

I PULLED ON MY hiking boots and headed out with my beloved dog to my daddy tree. As I walked along the forest trail, breathing in the fresh scents of the earth, sadness rolled through me in waves. Suddenly I was standing on the path in sunlight that shimmered through the trees. I paused and let the rays warm my face. I took a long, deep breath and calmly hiked on until the path took me around the hillside. My heart filled with joy when I saw my daddy tree.

"You're still here." I laughed out loud.

I ran over and wrapped my arms around our tree, smiling, with tears streaming down my face. I looked up into the high branches and heard "My beautiful Ber. I know you're sad that I died, but don't be too sad. You know why. I'll see you in the sky."

Epilogue

It has been eight months since my father passed. When I started writing my memoir over four years ago, I had no idea that I would be finishing the book just as my father took his last breath. Writing during these months has helped me face my sadness in the silence as I receive no more letters, no more cards, no more phone calls.

I know that I am fortunate to have had so much time with my father. I said everything I wanted and needed to say to him, and in that, I have completion. My love for Dad grew in the years we spent getting to know one another while he was incarcerated. I did not realize how much closer my father and I would become when I shared my true emotions with him. I am forever grateful for that, and I have written this book to share that heartening possibility with others.

I gained so much more than I lost, having the father I did.

My childhood was marked by violence, and my father was in prison for most of my life. These two facts led me to seek answers: I wanted to understand how I was shaped by the incidents that frightened and confused me.

Until I grew curious and took action to explore my unconscious self, I was unaware of how the stories I had spun to avoid feeling my underlying wounds were influencing my life. I began to realize how behaviors I adopted as a child—such as accommodating the needs of others rather than taking care of my own, desiring outside validation to prove I was lovable, and staying busy to avoid my emotions—were interfering with my relationships, especially the one I had with myself.

I used to imagine how much better my life would have been if my father hadn't done the things he did. I believed he caused my wounds. I thought that if he had been different, I wouldn't have to be doing all this healing work in the first place. I resented and blamed him. I was a victim.

Byron Katie says when you fight reality, you suffer. As I learned how to surrender to reality, how to let go of the judging belief that what happened shouldn't have happened, I stopped suffering. And I have to ask: If my father hadn't been who he was and done what he did, would I be the person I am today?

Today I take responsibility for who I am. I now am able to make life choices from a place of peace that doesn't blame others but understands that they act out of hurt and unconscious behaviors, just as I have done. Today I can almost always stop judging myself and other people by questioning my thoughts instead of worrying, instead of trying to control others to feel safer, instead of thinking I should have done more to meet someone's approval. I've learned that I deserve to be free from the suffering caused by my thoughts. And I can more easily accept all of my emotions, even the ones I used to avoid, like fear and sadness. I'm calmer and more trusting, knowing that I'm not alone. Today I know that I am connected with an immensely loving spirit that unites us all.

I always have been.

Acknowledgments

I am forever grateful for the people who have been by my side, living my story with me and supporting me in sharing it as I write this memoir.

My sister, Lyn, not only spent hours reading and editing preliminary drafts, but also had many conversations with me about our growing up together that helped me remember and relive those times we shared. My respect and fondness for her deepened during those conversations, as we opened even more to one another, talking about our experiences through the years being sisters. In writing about our lives together, I came to appreciate how much we have influenced each other, how we grew to be close and how we became strong and dynamic women because we had one another. With my sister's encouragement to keep writing and not give up, I was able to stay on track, and even when I didn't feel like it, I kept coming back.

I am deeply thankful for all the years of my mother's mentoring. She was and has been exactly the mother I needed in order to write this book, because she gave me the guidance that helped me know that I could do it. She believed in me.

Thanks to my children, Chavo, Sol and Jessica, for loving me in times of fun and times of struggle. I am so grateful for their unconditional support. My children fill my soul with joy and meaning. I am fortunate to be their mom. I have told the stories in these pages in the hopes that the telling will bring us closer as a family, giving my children a better understanding of where we came from and why certain things happened the way they did. I wanted them to know the truth.

I am grateful to Lonnie King for writing his beautiful letter to President Obama and for the use of it here.

I cannot fathom how I would have written this book without dedicated assistance from my writing and life coach, Maggie de Vries. Maggie appeared like magic one day, and I knew I had been given a gift. She has been the one reliable person who has held sacred space for me to write my memoir, no matter what. She guided me to the depths of my soul to bare it all, and then helped me through countless hours to learn how to write about it. With her patience and intuition, time and time again she pulled me through when I was emotionally stuck or discouraged about my writing abilities. She knew when to give me space and when to challenge me until, in the end, we got it done. We went to the moon and back.

Special thanks to those individuals who read the draft manuscript and gave me invaluable feedback: Flo Queen

Stover, Erica Brown, RV, Dr. Susan Allison, Wendy Morrison, Christina Gustafson and Jane Bernstein.

Thanks to Teresa Bubela for shepherding this project so lovingly through the printing process, and for her brilliant design. Because of her, *See You in the Sky* is beautiful to behold. Thanks to Audrey McClellan for her attention to detail and the great care and patience with which she copyedited my story, and thanks to Dawn Loewen, whose corrections and queries as proofreader made *See You in the Sky* stronger still. I am blessed to have such a devoted and skilled team on my first book.

Finally, thanks to my father, who continues to give me creative messages and loving encouragement from his soul in the sky.

Online Resources

Adult Children of Alcoholics/Dysfunctional Families (ACA)

adultchildren.org

A "Twelve Step, Twelve Tradition program [for] men and women who grew up in dysfunctional homes."

Big Brothers Big Sisters

bbbs.org

Caring adult role models for children and youth in communities across the country.

Center for Restorative Justice Works

crjw.us

"Re-weaves the web of relationships that have been torn apart by crime and the policies of the criminal justice system."

Child Welfare Information Gateway

childwelfare.gov

Comprehensive resources to help protect children and strengthen families.

#Cut50

cut50.org

A national initiative to reduce prison populations while making our communities safer.

Echoes of Incarceration

echoesofincarceration.org

"A documentary initiative produced by youth with incarcerated parents."

Foreverfamily

foreverfam.org

Services for children with incarcerated parents and their families.

Free America

letsfreeamerica.com

Founded by John Legend, a campaign to transform America's criminal justice system.

Get on the Bus Program (Center for Restorative Justice Works)

crjw.us/programs/get-on-the-bus/

Brings children and their caregivers from throughout California to visit mothers and fathers in prison.

National Mentoring Resource Center

nationalmentoringresourcecenter.org

Resources to help youth mentoring programs improve their services.

National Resource Center on Children and Families of the Incarcerated

nrccfi.camden.rutgers.edu

Raises awareness about needs of children and families of the incarcerated (e.g., by disseminating information, guiding policy development and training workers in the field).

Osborne Association

osborneny.org

"Works in partnership with individuals, families, and communities to create opportunities for people affected by the criminal justice system."

Project Avary

projectavary.org

"Offers long-term support, resources, guidance and training for children with incarcerated parents."

Save Kids of Incarcerated Parents

skipinc.org

Provides support services for children of incarcerated parents and their families and increases awareness through education, advocacy and research.

Sesame Workshop

sesameworkshop.org

The global nonprofit behind Sesame Street, "on a mission to help kids everywhere grow smarter, stronger, and kinder."

SUSU Network: See Us, Support Us

susu-osborne.org/join-the-susu-network

"National network of families affected by parental incarceration, advocates, service providers, allies, and more."

WEGOTUSNOW

wegotusnow.org

"A national movement, built by, led by and about children and young adults impacted by parental incarceration."

The Work of Byron Katie

thework.com

A practice that helps people question what they believe and find answers inside themselves.

Youth.gov

Federal website of resources to support organizations and community partnerships offering programs for youth.

As a passionate advocate for families affected by incarceration, **JERI ROSS** works to raise awareness of and funds for the hundreds of thousands of American children who have a parent in prison. She also serves on the advisory board for the Aztecas Youth Soccer Academy, a non-profit organization that mentors at-risk youth, providing a positive alternative to gangs and violent criminal behavior. Jeri is a Licensed Health Educator with a master's in public health. She is a speaker, an author and a motivational Life Coach, conducting one-on-one sessions and workshops that help people heal and lead happier, healthier lives.

Jeri works and plays on the beaches and redwood forest trails of Santa Cruz, California, with her beloved children, grandchildren, friends and faithful dog. For more information, visit **jerirossbefree.com**.